CW01064711

The History and Practice of Britain's Railways

The History and Practice of Britain's Railways

A New Research Agenda

Edited by
R.W. Ambler

Ashgate
Aldershot • Brookfield USA • Singapore • Sydney

Published by
Ashgate Publishing Limited
Gower House, Croft Road
Aldershot
Hants GU11 3HR
United Kingdom

Ashgate Publishing Company
Old Post Road
Brookfield
Vermont 05036-9704
USA

ISBN 1 84014 667 2

British Library Cataloguing-in-Publication Data
The History and Practice of Britain's Railways : A New Research Agenda
    1.Railroads - Great Britain - History - Congresses
    I.Ambler, R. W.
    385'.0941

US Library of Congress Cataloging-in-Publication Data
The History and practice of Britain's railways : a new research agenda /
    edited by R.W. Ambler.
       p.   cm.
    Includes bibliographical references and index
    1. Railroads--Great Britain--History. I. Ambler, R.W
    HE3018.H57 1999   98-46722
    285'.0941--dc21   CIP

Typeset in Times Roman by John Rickard

Printed in Great Britain by Galliards, Great Yarmouth

Contents

List of Tables and Figures

Plates

Abbreviations

BR	British Rail, British Railways
ECR	Eastern Counties Railway
ESRC	Economic & Social Research Council
GCR	Great Central Railway
GJC	Grand Junction Canal
GNR	Great Northern Railway
GSWR	Great Southern and Western Railway
GUC	Grand Union Canal
GWR	Great Western Railway
L&M	Liverpool & Manchester Railway
L&YR	Lancashire & Yorkshire Railway
LBR	London & Birmingham Railway
LMS	London, Midland & Scottish Railway
LNER	London & North Eastern Railway
LNWR	London & North Western Railway
LSR	Leicester & Swannington Railway
LSWR	London & South Western Railway
LTSR	London, Tilbury and Southend Railway
MCR	Midland Counties Railway
MGWR	Midland Great Western Railway
MMN	Melton Mowbray Navigation
MR	Midland Railway
MS&L	Manchester, Sheffield & Lincolnshire Railway
NCR	Newcastle & Carlisle Railway
NER	North Eastern Railway
NRM	National Railway Museum
NSR	North Staffordshire Railway
OUC	Old Union Canal
PP	Parliamentary Papers
PRO	Public Record Office
SBR	Shrewsbury and Birmingham Railway
TMC	Trent & Mersey Canal

Contributors

R.W.Ambler	Department of History, University of Hull
G.Biddle	Levens, near Kendal
D.Dilks	Vice-Chancellor, University of Hull
C.Divall	The Institute of Railway Studies, York
M.W.Kirby	Department of Economics, University of Lancaster
M.J.T.Lewis	Department of History,University of Hull
H.Newby	Vice-Chancellor, University of Southampton
M.C.Reed	Glasgow
D.Turnock	Department of Geography, University of Leicester

Foreword

David Dilks

The papers published in this collection were originally presented at a seminar held in the University of Hull in April 1995. All the participants, and now a wider community, are indebted to the Economic and Social Research Council for the grant (A4022264011) which made our gathering possible. Indeed, I should not like to content myself with a formal acknowledgement; the gathering owed a great deal to the enthusiasm of Professor Howard Newby, then Chief Executive of the ESRC and now Vice-Chancellor of the University of Southampton, an enthusiastic expert upon many aspects of British railways; and our indebtedness to him is compounded by the chapter which he has contributed to this volume.

Our seminar was characterized by a wide range of interests. Some 35 people attended. They included colleagues from 12 British universities, publishers and editors of books and journals, representatives of societies, individuals with a special interest in the subject. In sum, the mixture was not the same as at many gatherings held in universities; we represented the amateur as well as the professional study of railways, and it was hardly possible to be in the room without being reminded that 'amateur' means one who studies for love of a subject, not necessarily one who simply fails to attain the higher standard of the professionals.

Our gathering could not have been brought together without the encouragement of many friends of the University and of the subject. Although he was unable to attend, Professor Jack Simmons provided invaluable advice from the earliest stages of its planning, while Professors Jay Appleton and Allan Patmore of the University of Hull also gave considerable support and encouragement to Professor Howell Lloyd and Dr Rod Ambler who were responsible for its arrangements. They in their turn acknowledged the invaluable assistance which they received in the organisation of the seminar from the excellent staff in the office of the Department of History at Hull, and the strong support which they enjoyed from the Head of Department, Mr John Bernasconi.

The seminar programme was divided into three main sessions under the general heads of economic and social history, historical geography, and technology and railway development. These were chaired by Dr Gordon Jackson of the University of Strathclyde, Professor Jay Appleton, and Professor Colin Russell of the Open University, each of whom, as well as playing a central role through their contribution to these parts of the day's proceedings, also gave generous assistance in their planning. Two of the contributors - Dr Terry Gourvish of the Business History Unit at the London School of Economics and Dr John Farrington of the University of Aberdeen - did not bring forward their papers for publication.

We had opportunities for discussion after each of the three main sessions of the seminar. In addition, we were all conscious of the contribution which can be, indeed regularly is, made by people who are not professionally engaged in the study of railway history, and of the contribution which that interest will provide to a new research agenda. Accordingly, the members of the seminar divided into discussion groups led by chairmen from the world of railway publishing: Mr Michael Blakemore of *Backtrack*, Mr David Jenkinson of the Pendragon Partnership and Mr Peter Semmens of the *Railway Magazine*. At the end of the day, we discussed under Professor Newby's chairmanship the main issues which had been identified.

There was a general sense of common purpose, and we all felt a desire to give a wider circulation to the papers which had been presented, and to stimulate a broader and serious debate. Hence the publication of this book, which has been prepared as camera ready copy by Mr John Rickard, a postgraduate student in the Department of History here.

I take this opportunity to express warm thanks to Dr Ambler for all the care which he lavished upon the organisation of the seminar, and has now brought to bear upon the editing of this book.

Chapter One

Antiquarianism or Analysis? The Future of Railway History

Howard Newby

This book is in itself an accident of history. Its immediate origins lie in a set of papers submitted to a conference held at the University of Hull in April 1995 on 'The History and Practice of Britain's Railways: A New Research Agenda'. The conference brought together a wide ranging group of professional and amateur historians, academic specialists in railway history, representatives from the worlds of railway preservation and railway publishing and a small group of people who, like myself, could only be described as railway enthusiasts. The Conference was generously supported by the Economic and Social Research Council (of which I had ceased to be Chief Executive in 1994) and was marked by a clear spirit of collegiality across participants coming from wide-ranging backgrounds.

The purpose of the conference was to assess the current state of railway history in the United Kingdom and to indicate the ways in which the research base of railway historiography could be strengthened and improved in the future. There was a general consensus that railway history, like the nostalgia which underpins the burgeoning railway preservation movement, is not what it used to be. Indeed it was widely regarded as being in the doldrums. This contrasts with the increasing interest shown in railway journalism, the railway preservation movement, and other associated aspects of 'railway heritage' which are booming, fuelled no doubt by the increased disposable income of a postwar generation of schoolboy railway enthusiasts who have now reached middle age and a level of disposable income which allows them to support, railwayana auctions, the purchase of magazines and books and other tangible aspects of the contemporary railway heritage scene.

These factors bore upon the very particular set of circumstances which led to the establishment of the seminar, the accident of history referred to above. In October 1993 the Director of the Science Museum, Neil Cossons, gave an unscripted after-dinner speech at a National Railway Museum (NRM) symposium in York. In his speech Cossons, whose responsibilities include the overall direction of the National Railway Museum, asked a series of searching questions about the nature of railway preservation in this country. His comments caused - and were almost certainly designed to cause - controversy.

With his tongue only slightly in his cheek he referred to the 'harmless' nature of railway preservationists, whose hobby he compared with keeping a cat. There were some distance echoes of the popular caricature of the anorak-clad trainspotter now transmogrified into a middle-aged railway preservationist, a 'harmless hobby which ... can give an enormous amount of pleasure to its participants, keeps people off the streets, but, I suggest, has little significance beyond that' (Cossons 1994, p.26).

More seriously he drew a sharp distinction between what he regarded as the serious business of the preservation of railway artefacts and what passed for 'preservation' on the many preserved railways which have sprung up across the country over the last thirty years. He wondered whether any preserved railway authentically reproduced the operations and artefacts of the steam railway era. Then he went on to question whether many so called 'preserved' railways represented preservation at all. As he put it in the subsequent written version, 'In my address I suggested that an important goal for the preservation movement would be to preserve and operate a railway to absolutely authentic historical and technical standards, in terms of real estate, locomotives and rolling stock, and methods of operation, so that the public at large would gain an accurate insight into, so to speak, a working time capsule of the railway and its history. I am not aware that such a railway exists.....' (Cossons 1994, p.26).

His comments were met with a storm of outrage in the railway press and beyond. *Steam Railway* magazine in particular took up the cudgels on behalf of the railway preservation movement. Its editor, Nigel Harris, described Cossons' speech as 'such a farrago of nonsense that it's difficult to know where to begin answering it' (Harris 1994, p.6). In more measured terms, David Morgan, Chairman of the Association of Railway Preservation Societies, concluded that Cossons 'could not be more wrong' (Morgan 1993, p.21). Many of these comments were echoed in the letter columns of subsequent issues.

These exchanges were more concerned with personal abuse than serious debate, but, fleetingly, some of the more serious issues could be glimpsed. Cossons alluded to these in a follow-up article, 'Railway Preservation: Whither or Wither?', published in *Steam Railway* in January 1994. In this he pointed to the contrast between the growing railway enthusiasts movement and the fact that 'there is now virtually no scholarly research or publication'. Rather than satisfying 'rigorous intellectual standards' and consciously aiming to 'explain, educate and interpret to a wide audience', railway preservation had come 'primarily to satisfy an internalist hobby interest rather than serve an externalist public good'. As a result railway history was in 'serious, if not terminal, decline'. The nub of Cossons' complaint therefore was that, 'The movement is narrow and sectarian in outlook and concentrates only on those aspects of so-called preservation that appeal to its participants, to the almost complete exclusion of others. There is no visible foundation in scholarship or published research. Railway history is not highly regarded or even recognised in the broad spectrum of historical studies and there is no obvious advancement of knowledge, or interpretation to a wider audience' (Cossons 1994, p.26).

At this point I have to insert a personal note. At the time of Cossons' speech I was Chief Executive of the Economic and Social Research Council (ESRC), the Government body responsible for funding, amongst other things, the academic study of economic and social history in Britain's universities. In this professional role I was aware that the serious study of railway history in the United Kingdom could hardly be described as being in a thriving state. It contrasted badly with both other aspects of transport history in the United Kingdom (most notably maritime and aviation history) and also with railway history in other countries, most notably Continental Europe and the United States. I was also struck by the number of the themes which had emerged in the correspondence in *Steam Railway*, some of which I believed to be misplaced. For example, it was clear that as far as the debate was concerned, railway history was characterized almost wholly by artefacts, (principally by locomotives and rolling stock) and a detailed, albeit knowledgeable, concern with appearances, as the ever controversial topic of locomotive liveries illustrates only too well.

As I pointed out in a subsequent letter to *Steam Railway* this concern with appearance, whilst valuable in itself, is not a substitute for serious historical analysis. 'Evocation', I wrote, 'is only a part of understanding, not the whole story. It should not be mistaken for analysis and synthesis which enables us to ask not only "what?" but "how?" and "why?" '. Indeed, I argued, railway preservation stands in relation to railway history rather like the activities of Victorian natural historians stands in relation to the science of molecular biology: an activity from which serious scientific study has drawn strength, but not to be confused with the real thing. This therefore raised the broader question of how the undoubted enthusiasm, seriousness and energy of the railway preservation movement could be harnessed to support and enhance the research base of railway history in this country (Newby 1994, p.22).

I offered, through the ESRC, to fund a conference examining these issues. Hence, interested parties were gathered together on a sunny Spring Saturday in Hull in April 1995. The papers presented at the conference, including those reproduced in this book, therefore attempted to achieve two aims. In part they were exemplars of what serious railway history might look like, and therefore, quite legitimately, the papers featured very particular topics or themes as a way of illustrating what is possible. The speakers also, however, all addressed bigger issues of how railway history could be better organized, supported and institutionalized. In this the then very recent creation of the Institute of Railway Studies at the University of York, (supported, it should be noted, by the National Railway Museum), was undoubtedly a major step forward. Colin

Divall, its founding Director was an active participant at the conference and contributes one of the chapters in this book. Undoubtedly the establishment of the Institute was an event of very great significance. Its mission not only to support serious academic study through its close links with the National Railway Museum, but also to extend its ambit into lifelong learning through offering a range of courses, will undoubtedly have a major influence over time on the character and progress of railway history in this country. But at the time of the conference the Institute remained in very embryonic form and, therefore, the discussions which took place in Hull were able to assist Professor Divall and his colleagues in developing their own priorities for the Institute.

It should be emphasized that the Conference did not seek to be prescriptive. It did not attempt, in any specific way, to propose particular topics for study, nor to recommend any particular approach to the study of railway history. Rather, the conference concerned itself with a number of broader, more abstract issues: railway historiography rather than railway history. It is impossible to do justice here to the full flavour of the discussions; but some themes were discernible.

First, there was consideration of why railway history was something of a backwater in British historical studies more generally. The general consensus was that it was not a particularly innovative or exciting part of the academic history scene and that few railway historians had developed ideas and insights which had contributed to the development of British history more generally. On the whole, railway history was portrayed, despite some notable exceptions, as dull, descriptive and bordering on the antiquarian. Good histories of railway companies, railway operating, and the economic and social impacts of railways did exist, but in general they had failed to keep pace with the approaches and issues which has enlivened historical studies more generally over the last two decades. There was probably a need for old histories to be revisited and for new areas of study to be opened up. As already indicated above this contrasted markedly with the state of another kind of railway history, associated with the railway preservation movement, historical modelling etc. The latter is supported by a wide and burgeoning commercial press, where the standards of publishing, in both magazines and books, has improved remarkably. There is also a burgeoning network of associations and societies, such as the Historical Model Railway Society, LMS society, LNER society, etc. which has brought together the amateur hobby interests of tens of thousands of people interested in the history of our railways. The interest was certainly there, and was, not least, being successfully commercially exploited. Why, then, did this not filter through into the more serious and analytical study of railway history?

One possibility, and it had to be faced, was that Neil Cossons may, in certain respects, have been correct. Was the success of railway history in inverse relationship to the growth of railway preservation and railway enthusiasm more generally? Perhaps, it was argued, that serious students of railway history, not least those seeking to undertake a Ph.D in university history departments, were being put off the subject by its 'image problem' - the 'anorak' trainspotters as referred to above. Some of the correspondence following Neil Cossons' speech gave a certain amount of credence to this. The assertions of what railway modellers call 'rivet counters' - i.e., those with an almost obsessional concern for the detailed appearance of railway artefacts - seemed at times to suggest that in their view, this *was* railway history and that little more needed to be said. This concern with appearance and operating procedure, on which the railway modelling press understandably concentrates, does indeed seem to carry with it a distant, middle-aged echo of schoolboy trainspotting.

Now clearly the preservation of artefacts and their appearance has its place. But we should recognize it for what it is. As an end in itself it constitutes little more than antiquarianism: no harm in that, but it is not analytical social and economic history. Asking the 'what' questions is a necessary first step and any historian would begin with the recoverable facts. But it is *only* a first step. Serious historians will also ask a set of 'why' questions and this forms a basis of a true analysis. Hence the obsession with the directly observable may well have hindered the development of a deeper more analytical approach to railway history which could inform us not only of the understanding of railways themselves, but also contribute to broader issues in the development of British historiography. It is this set of analytical issues which railway history has in general, in this country, failed to come up with.

The development of this kind of agenda needs more than an initial interest in railway artefacts. It requires, as I stated in my contribution to the debate in *Steam Railway*, time, talent and training. It also requires a certain amount of national and regional organization. For example, there is a clear need to coordinate and integrate the efforts and interests of the many thousands of dedicated railway enthusiasts and amateur historians with the professional analytical skills of academic specialists. One important bridge between the two, which was discussed at the conference, is the railway press and in particular the kind of intelligent railway journalism epitomized by magazines such as *Backtrack*, and high quality publishers such as Wild Swan and the Oakwood Press. Such popular railway publishing outlets provide both an opportunity and an incentive for the dedicated enthusiast to engage in detailed, painstaking, and often local historical research which can form the raw material of broader, more analytical historical research and writing.

It is by no means impossible to envisage this broad spectrum of interests and aptitudes becoming the basis for a much more sustained, and enriched, 'new railway history'. It has, after all, succeeded elsewhere: for example, in areas as diverse as population and landscape history, where respectively local, even parochial, population studies and the presentation of countryside and gardens (often via the National Trust) have fed the academic research agenda to the mutual benefit of the gifted amateur and the experienced professional. But this does require both resources and a modicum of management. This is most obviously apparent in the provision of training. The enthusiastic amateur requires some training in the handling of archives and other source material. To sift the available evidence and construct a robust argument on the basis of incomplete material requires a degree of tuition and mentoring.

All of this implies the provision of some kind of infrastructure in research training and research support. The Institute of Railway Studies clearly has the potential to fulfil a national coordinating role. But in an era of distance learning and lifelong learning, it is not too difficult to envisage a national network of adult research training opportunities based around professionally led local or regional research programmes. The resource base is also beginning to be made more accessible, thanks in part to developments in information technologies. In addition to familiar sources, such as the NRM and the Public Record Office (PRO), other resources, such as the Historical Model Railway Society's new centre at Butterley in Derbyshire, point the way ahead towards the integrated provision of archives, libraries and study space. Even the prospect of National Lottery funding could make this more than a mere pipe dream.

The development of this kind of institutional base would transform the prospects for railway history, while bringing together the amateur and the professional in potentially exciting new ways. Professional historians necessarily go through a lengthy period of rigorous research training, usually to Ph.D and beyond. This not only involves the ability to make use of archives and to gather and analyse large amounts of sometimes quantitative information, but also involves a much broader intellectual training so that they are asking the right kinds of analytical questions of the material they have gathered. But this is in no way decries the efforts and enthusiasm of so many amateur, usually local, historians who have contributed so much, not only to the preservation of materials and archives but also to the knowledge base of particular aspects of railway history. Harnessing this talent and enthusiasm is one of the great challenges ahead. But it will not in itself be sufficient. Railway historians need to ask some big questions and not just a series of little ones. It is only then, perhaps, that the attention of a wider historical community can be captured and that the sense of excitement which is so apparent amongst the large majority of railway enthusiasts can be repeated among the professional students of railway history in the United Kingdom. This book is a modest contribution to that aim.

Chapter Two

Railway Investment

M. C. Reed

It may appear presumptuous for someone who has long since ceased to wander in this particular grove of academe to offer, even by invitation, an overview of historical research on railway investment. I am very conscious of this, and of the fact that I have not had an opportunity to review much of the more recent literature, so I must apologize in advance for the gaps in my coverage of the material, and to those whose work I may have unintentionally overlooked. I have also to acknowledge an ambiguity, both in the title of my paper and in my approach to its subject. 'Investment' is a word which it is easy to overuse, but while a purist may insist on restricting the term to the act of capital formation, it is also a convenient shorthand for the financial process of recruiting and applying savings. Though much of what I have to say falls within the latter usage, and deals with investment in railways, in attempting to set out my perception of the relevance of this specific area of study I shall also inevitably need to mention the outcomes of this process, the effects of investment by railways. The nexus between saving and investment is, of course, a central theme in economics, and Britain's experience of building up its railway system during the nineteenth century provides some useful insights into this process.

*
* *

Contemporaries were well aware of the uniqueness of the great mid-nineteenth century wave of investment in railways in Britain, and its contribution to the transformation of the economic, social and physical fabric of Victorian Britain. From parliamentary sources and other enquiries they were able to establish its scale with some precision, and to attempt analyses which went beyond the popular pathologies of the Railway Mania. Against the more arresting titles such as *The Bubble of the Age* (Smith 1848) and *How He reigned and How He Mizzled* (Crowquill 1849), or even the high tone of Herbert Spencer (1854), we can set the painstaking collation of data by practitioners such as Scrivenor (1849) and the objectivity of Tooke's and Newmarch's account of the financial background to the Mania years (Tooke and Newmarch 1838–57). The later economic historian who seeks to survey this field has the benefit not only of expert contemporary commentators, but also a rich vein of company and parliamentary records, supplemented by a financial press which largely owed its creation to the public interest in railway investment and which remains invaluable to our understanding of the context in which such investment took place.

Despite this wealth of material, and the references to railway development in many general studies and even in some theoretical works, the systematic modern investigation of railway investment in nineteenth century Britain dates back little more than forty years. During the 1950s, pioneering studies by Pollins (1952, 1954, 1957–58) and Broadbridge (1955, 1957) began to explore the railway capital market beyond the level of generalization which had characterized much previous comment; in the same decade, work by Matthews (1954) and Hughes (1960) placed railway investment within rigorous analyses of its macro economic framework, respectively covering the years 1833–42 and 1850–60. These studies were followed by Mitchell's (1964) and Kenwood's (1965) refinement of the raw investment data into a form which enabled its relationship to national economic indicators, first considered by Cairncross (1953) and Feinstein (1961), to be stated with more precision and over a longer period. Others carried forward the work on the structure of the capital market which had begun during the 1950s, while company studies such as those by Channon (1972) and Irving (1971, 1976) examined influences affecting individual investment decisions. At a wider level, Hawke (1970) and Vamplew (1971) applied in a British context the techniques which had been pioneered in Fishlow's (1965) and Fogel's (1964) work on the consequences of railway investment in the USA. By 1980 several valuable syntheses had been published which gave due weight to recent work on railway investment (Pollins 1971; Bagwell 1974; Gourvish 1980), presenting a more rounded picture than had previously been available either in general economic histories or in the more specialist literature.

*
* *

In common with other fields of scholarship, the study of economic history has its own intrinsic interest and subjective value for those who undertake it. But while that may be sufficient motivation for current amateurs such as myself, it is hardly an adequate justification for research funding bodies to have sponsored the broad swathe of work which since the 1950s has expanded our knowledge of the processes of railway investment. In venturing some rather more objective reasons for this interest, perhaps I can also suggest some areas of continuing relevance.

As Terry Gourvish has aptly observed, before the First World War the railways were among Britain's leading half dozen industries (Gourvish 1980, p.10). And, while much of the thrust of the econometric approach to the history of the railways has been to question some of the previous generalizations about the economic consequences of their introduction, Gary Hawke had no difficulty in subscribing to the proposition that 'railways had the greatest impact of any single innovation in Britain in the nineteenth century' (Hawke and Reed 1969, p.269). So long as there is a place for the academic study of modern British economic history - and I have a firm personal belief in its didactic value - there is as strong a case for attempting to explore further the functioning of the railway industry as there is for continuing analysis of the other great Victorian staples, such as cotton, coal and iron and steel. If such an argument might seem somewhat narrow and tending towards historical determinism, it is worth returning to a point that I have already touched upon. The experience of railway development in the nineteenth century has been used to inform significant areas of economic debate, and indeed finds a contemporary political echo in some of the current controversy about railway privatization. Borrowing again from Terry Gourvish, he reminded me long ago of the frequency of the appeal to history: the corollary is that it is important that such history should be well-informed if it is to be used to support other conclusions.

The second main reason why the history of railway investment in Britain has provided a focus for research concentrates more narrowly on the investment process itself. Again, it brings us to the interface between history and economics, into an area that has its own historiographical interest: the interaction between capital formation and economic growth. If there was a single 'big idea' that was instrumental in placing this theme firmly on the scholarly agenda, it was undoubtedly Rostow's (1960) enunciation of the theory in *The Stages of Economic Growth* that a threshold level of investment was required to trigger the take-off into sustained economic growth. Its publication in 1960 was itself sufficient to stimulate vigorous debate among economists and historians, and many of Rostow's findings were almost immediately challenged or refined.[1] In a sense, this was probably immaterial to the significance of the work: its antecedents in the collaborative *Growth and Fluctuation of the British Economy* (Gayer, Rostow and Schwartz 1953) provided vindication for those who saw economic history as the laboratory of the social sciences, and it is tempting, though doubtless entirely frivolous, to suggest that the approach encapsulated by Rostow may have itself have generated something of a take-off in the study of economic history in Britain. It is certainly interesting, however, to observe the juxtaposition of a persuasive theoretical imperative and the post Robbins growth in the number of separate university departments of economic history.

I have already implied that the immediate significance of Rostow's work

---

[1]   An invaluable summary is provided in the introduction to Crouzet (1972).

lay not so much in its detail but in its articulation of a paradigm. The debate about the detail began immediately, and, paradoxically, it was this debate that refocused attention on the role of railways. Rostow himself had described railroads as 'historically the most powerful single initiator of take-offs' (Rostow 1960, pp.302–3), but he argued that in Britain 'take-off' levels of investment – that is over ten per cent of national income – had been reached during the late eighteenth century (Crouzet 1972, pp.11–12). However, reworking of the historical data led in particular by Deane (Crouzet 1972, pp.14–26; Deane and Cole 1964, pp. 259–64, 269–77, 303–9), had the effect of suggesting the early railway age as the period when such investment levels were probably first attained in Britain. This finding in itself had wider implications for the 'take-off' argument, since Britain was by then clearly established as an industrial nation, and the debate has subsequently been still further refined, both in terms of the data employed and in terms of its theoretical basis (Gourvish 1980, p.33). But the initial unfolding of these wider arguments about capital formation gave an additional stimulus to studies of the railway investment process in Britain, and helps to provide a wider context for such studies.

Indeed, in terms of this context, the development of the British railway system is probably the first example of a single industrial sector with investment requirements that were large enough to be significant in macro economic terms, and these requirements were a direct consequence of the nature of railway technology. The form of the rails that were necessary to carry a steam locomotive resulted in a total interrelatedness between vehicles and track, and this distinguishes railways from any other mode of transport in general use. The specialized nature of even the most primitive steam railways required capital to be sunk in a complete system between two traffic centres before any worthwhile revenue could be earned; and the scale of the outlay on land, engineering, track, terminals and rolling stock that was required for even a modest line was such that the railways quickly outclassed any other category of joint stock undertaking in terms of their demands on the capital market Over roughly a century of development in Britain canal companies raised a total share capital of less than £20 million (Spackman 1843, p.157); railway companies in England raised more than £40 million from shares between 1820 and 1844 alone (Hawke and Reed 1969, p.270). By 1881 the paid-up capital of British railways exceeded the funded National Debt, and the railways were by then also investing a significant proportion of their annual earnings in maintaining their capital stock.

*

* *

The pattern of railway investment and its relations with the fluctuations of the wider economy are now well known. There was a rapid initial acceleration, from under £500,000 in 1831 to about £9 million at the end of that decade. After falling to an annual rate of under £4 million during the early 1840s, investment peaked at over £30 million in 1847 before declining again to around £8.5 million during the early 1850s. The next peak, of about £24 million, came in 1866 and expenditure continued to vary significantly throughout the next half century, with annual levels ranging from less than £12 million to more than £20 million (Kenwood 1965, pp. 313–22; Mitchell 1964, pp. 315–36).

These variations in railway investment conformed broadly with the outline of the trade cycle. At times the relationship was weak: the economic recovery in 1853 was barely reflected in railway investment, which was still influenced by the reaction to the Railway Mania, while the trough of 1894 was a faintly discernible interruption in a long upswing that peaked in 1900. In contrast, during some stages of the initial development of the network, changes in the level of railway investment activity were strong enough to affect the general economic cycle. In the mid 1830s, and even more so in the 1840s, enthusiasm for railway promotion contributed significantly to economic optimism in the upswing, and the volumes of investment generated by these promotional booms had the effect of ensuring that railway capital spending continued at a high level during the succeeding depressions.

In real terms, the level of investment attained during the 1840s was unique in British railway history, and it is to these years in particular that attention has turned when assessing the role of the railways in gross domestic capital formation. While the optimism which led up to the Railway Mania quickly turned into excess and was followed by a collapse of confidence in the autumn of 1845, capital expenditure did not reach its maximum until 1847 because of the lags inherent in the authorization and construction processes. The consensus is that in that year UK railway investment accounted for almost 7 per cent of national income, and more than 40 per cent of total gross domestic capital formation (Gourvish 1980, p.13).

The implications of this concentration of investment were debated by contemporaries, and have been revisited by a number of subsequent analysts. One interpretation has emphasized the distortion of other expenditure patterns that resulted from the demands for funds which railways made upon investors, many of whom were locked into their commitments by the fall in share prices that followed the collapse of the Mania. In this analysis, railway investment is seen as contributing to the financial crisis of 1847 and to the scale of the associated depression.[2] The other interpretation stresses instead the beneficial effects of railway demand in an otherwise depressed economy: Mitchell estimated that railway construction alone employed around 4 per cent of the

---

[2] See Hawke (1970), pp.364–5.

working male population in 1847, and that railway demand for iron from 1844 to 1851 was equivalent to almost 18 per cent of the UK's total pig iron output (Mitchell 1964, pp. 322–5). As Hawke has pointed out, however, these opposing views can be partially reconciled by taking account of the lags between the *raising* of capital and its *expenditure*, and by noting the phased impact of railway investment on different sectors of the economy (Hawke 1970, pp. 365–70). On this basis, it is possible to accept not only that the railways' requirements for funds contributed to the crisis of 1847, but also that the expenditure for which this finance was required was ultimately beneficial because of the economic stimulus which it gave during the depression.

Railway promotion overreached itself to such an extent during the mid 1840s that almost two decades elapsed before there was a comparable boom. Investment expenditure during both 1865 and 1866 was over £23 million, the highest level since 1848. However, railway investment during the 1860s was proportionately less significant than during the 1840s, because of the general growth of the economy during the intervening period: at its peak in 1866 railway investment amounted to under 3 per cent of UK national income and to less than a third of total domestic fixed capital formation. And while the financial crisis of 1866 was followed by a sharp decline in railway capital expenditure, the recovery was not delayed, as it had been during the 1850s. There was a significant new upswing after 1869 and though fluctuations in investment expenditure remained evident thereafter, they were generally less extreme. This was partly because renewal expenditure, which was largely autonomous, accounted for a greater proportion of gross railway investment as the system entered a more mature stage. Indeed, there is some evidence from around the turn of the century that a few of the larger companies followed a consciously contra cyclical policy for some of their renewals, for example by increasing major locomotive overhauls during periods of slack trade. For reasons to which I shall return later, another factor was also of relevance in damping some of the fluctuations in new capital expenditure: this was the growing weight of the large amalgamated undertakings in the total picture.

*
* *

After this cursory look at the overall pattern of railway investment, and the even briefer reference to some of its immediate economic outcomes during the later 1840s, I should like now to turn to the supply side, the means by which capital was mobilized for this investment, and comment briefly on a number of aspects before offering some thoughts about possible future avenues of exploration.

If British railway investment during the later 1840s was of a dimension sufficient to register on the Rostovian scale, how significant were the levels of saving that were required to finance this investment? When I first considered the savings issue in relation to the immediately preceding period, that from 1825 to 1844, my conclusion then was that, despite the extraordinary focusing of investors' attention on railways, the total sums that were required were not out of proportion to other demands which the British economy had been able to sustain (Reed 1975, pp.44–51). If one considers railway capital requirements together with the sums that were raised for foreign loans or the resources that had been required to sustain the Napoleonic wars (including their domestic consequence of investment in the agricultural sector to enable the latter to increase its output), it is evident that there was no overall shortage of capital in Britain in the first half of the nineteenth century. Indeed, the picture suggested by national debt reductions and generally declining yields on Consols during the 1820s and 1830s is supplemented by insurance company records which confirm instead the relative paucity of profitable investment outlets (Reed 1975, pp.242–3). And while the events of 1847 may suggest that, at their height, railway demands could have disturbed the circulation of capital, the effects of contemporary events in Ireland, and the need for the export of specie to pay for grain imports, should not be forgotten. Taking the long view, it seems clear that investment in domestic railways was just one of a succession of financial opportunities which attracted the attention of British capitalists in the century before the First World War. The home railways' later complaints about the difficulty of raising capital, far from being evidence of a shortage of investible funds, confirmed instead the competitive nature of the capital market within which they found themselves operating.

However, one of the features of early railway investment seems to have been that it attracted funds from sources which had not previously participated, at least to such an extent, in the formal capital market. This had two important consequences. This wider participation must, prima facie, have increased the total availability of investible funds, while the transformation of the institutional apparatus of the capital market that was so clearly associated with this process helped to improve its efficiency, creating a more perfect market. Again, both of these aspects have now become a commonplace, but it is worth restating the outline of these developments.

So far as the sources of capital for early railway development are concerned, pace Evans, and to some extent Clapham (Evans 1936, p.10; Clapham 1964, p.386), it is hoped that the myth of the locally financed early railway has now been laid to rest. While parliamentary processes, through the recitation of the names of leading subscribers in early railway bills and through the device of the subscription contract, may have appeared to place a premium on the close identification of financial interest in a project with local benefit, the requirement to have a given percentage of funding in place before a bill could proceed through its Commons and then its Lords stages had the opposite effect.

Analyses of those early railway schemes for which evidence has survived clearly demonstrate the insufficiency of local funding, and the need to tap other sources, whether through the Quaker network that was used to part finance the Stockton & Darlington Railway (Kirby 1993, pp.47–53; Reed 1975, pp.169–78), or the London money that was drawn upon to complete the subscriptions to the Liverpool & Manchester (L&M) and Newcastle & Carlisle (NCR) (Pollins 1952, pp.90–7; Reed 1975, pp.118–26, 178–84). At times the means by which these non local subscribers were recruited were highly personalized, ranging, for example, from the marriage and business links which formed part of the close bonds within the Society of Friends, or a son's apprenticeship which brought a north country recusant landowner into the circle of investors which George Stephenson used to support the Leicester & Swannington Railway (Reed 1968, pp.10–20), to Saunder's often quoted 'sad, harassing work' in 'calling upon and pressing perfect strangers to contribute' to the Great Western Railway (GWR) (MacDermot 1964, p.11). But railways also seem to have found ready support in the fringe markets of the London stock exchange even when they were relatively unknown, as was evidenced by the company promotion boom of the mid 1820s (Reed 1975, pp.4–5, 16).

A similar picture prevailed during the first half of the 1830s, though modified by the fact that the successful opening of the Liverpool & Manchester Railway generated an enthusiasm for railway investment in Lancashire which spread far beyond the local network. While by noting that the London & Birmingham Railway (LBR) completed the trunk route from Lancashire to London it is possible to rationalize the fact that Liverpool supplied more of the initial capital for this line than the two cities named in its title, a similar explanation cannot be valid for the London & Southampton Railway, where 40 per cent of initial capital was supplied from Manchester (Reed 1975, pp.138–44, 147–52).

Stock Exchange interest in railway projects did not, of course, disappear during the railway boom of the mid 1830s. Indeed, it found expression in some 'London lines' such as the North Midland Railway or the Preston & Wyre (Reed 1975, pp.102n, 163), the latter in the Lancashire heartland of the new generation of railway capitalists. But the distinguishing feature of the wave of railway investment which took place during the 1830s is its close identification with Liverpool and Manchester, and further evidence that radical changes were taking place in the formal capital market is provided by the establishment there of the first two provincial stock exchanges in 1836 (Reed 1975, p.215). The influence of the railways on the financial markets during the 1830s and 1840s is emphasized still more by the emergence of a specialist press dedicated to railway investment matters; by the development of stockbroking as a trade in most towns; and by the creation of trading floors in virtually every major city during the boom of the 1840s (Reed 1975, pp.217–18). The scale of railway issues and the widespread dissemination of information about them effectively created the nineteenth-century share market, radically altering the business of the London Stock Exchange, and providing the stimulus for a network of provincial exchanges and brokers which extended opportunities for share transactions throughout the country.

The dispersal of railway share ownership, evident from the earliest days of publicly floated steam railways, was reinforced by this process: by 1902 there were over 700,000 separate holdings of shares in British railway companies (Railway News 1914, p.36), typically quite small: average holdings in most companies were under £1,500 (PP 1902 XC, p.889). And while some regional loyalty usually remained evident, surviving records suggest that local interests did not predominate. In 1860, for example, more than 40 per cent of a sample of the shareholders of the South Eastern Railway lived in Lancashire or Cheshire, compared with around a quarter in London, Kent and Sussex (South Eastern Railway 1860). Irving's sample of shareholders in the North Eastern Railway (NER) in 1921 shows less than a half living in the counties served by the line, despite the company's strong regional identity (Irving 1976, p.156). I have myself recently been taking a very preliminary look at the addresses of Highland Railway shareholders in 1913 by sampling pages in an address list of 262 pages containing almost 6000 names (Highland Railway 1913). Despite the accident of a random number generator which twice landed me among the 'Macs', in a 5 per cent sample there were more shareholders with addresses in England than north of the Tay.

*

* *

This close interrelationship between the railways and the development of the formal apparatus of the stock market is not surprising. Volume is crucial to the maintenance of liquidity in a securitized capital market, and railways provided the first example of joint stock enterprise on a sufficient scale to create a national market in such shares. This leads me to the next aspect that I wish to address: the efficiency of this new market and the nature of its relationships with the railway investment process, including the role of 'manias' in the development of the railway system.

It appears that, from an impressively early stage, the stock market was extremely effective at reflecting investors' expectations in a way which directly influenced companies' ability to raise funds and that, in these terms, a relatively perfect market soon developed (Anderson and Wynn 1975). Again, this is an area where the consequences for the railways have become more widely recognized as a result of the accumulation of research findings. There is an acute irony in the fact that this market, which the railways had largely created, so quickly became an obstacle to their easy raising of additional equity capital, forcing an early dependence on fixed interest funds. At first, loan capital provided the main source of supplementary funding, allowing the railways to tap the more traditional capital market that existed in the banks and insurance companies. However, growing financial sophistication and the legal restraints on borrowing soon led to the emergence of prior charge share issues. These, and the widespread adoption during the 1860s of perpetual debenture stocks in place of redeemable borrowing instruments, resulted in a convergence between the markets for loan and fixed dividend share capital, and left equities in the minority: in 1900 ordinary shares accounted for only 38 per cent of British railway capital (*Railway Returns* 1906 pp.xxvi–xxvii).

Moreover, the statutory restrictions on borrowing, and the long-standing objection of parliament to the payment of interest on calls on ordinary shares out of capital, placed new companies at a particular disadvantage in the mature capital market (PP 1882 XIII, p.635). As I have already suggested, this was one factor which contributed to the dampening of the fluctuations in new capital expenditure after the 1860s. Though the state of the stock market influenced existing companies' ability – or willingness – to raise fresh funds, they were able to fine tune their approach to the market in raising what were in any event usually relatively small additions to an established capital. The increasing dominance of the large amalgamated companies, and the decreasing scope for new undertakings to play a significant role, accordingly reduced the scale of fluctuations in investment.

The vulnerability of new companies was probably most strikingly demonstrated during the late 1850s and early 1860s, when the difficulties of the railway new issue market led to the emergence of the phenomenon of the 'contractor's line' (Pollins 1957–58). Cottrell has shown that much of the finance for such undertakings was indirectly raised through the short term money markets that were burgeoning as a result of contemporary changes in the structure of bill broking (Cottrell 1976). Even before the Overend, Gurney collapse had demonstrated the flimsiness of the credit pyramids that supported these activities, the *Railway Times* was condemning the 'jobbers' who were seeking to blackmail the established companies through such promotions (*Railway Times* 1865, pp.1166–7, 1226). And while the attention of historians has largely focused on the means by which the physical construction of contractors' lines was financed, there is another aspect that might perhaps repay further examination: the parallel role of hire and finance companies in the provision of rolling stock for those railways which were unable to raise sufficient of their own capital for this purpose. This was by no means a short lived phenomenon: the establishment of the Railway Rolling Stock Trust in 1896 was one of the ways in which the hopelessly over extended Manchester Sheffield & Lincolnshire Railway (MS&L) was able to sustain its push towards

London in the face of the exhaustion of its capital powers and the justified scepticism of the Stock Exchange (Dow 1962, pp.277, 287).

But if stock market conditions were so pervasive an influence on the exercise of railway companies' capital powers, affecting the financial policies of even the soundest companies (Irving 1976, pp.114–17), to what extent was railway investment simply a dependent variable of stock exchange conditions? In particular, were the great peaks of railway investment in the 1830s and 1840s purely, to borrow Keynes's redolent expression, 'the by-product of the activities of a casino' (Keynes 1973, p.159)?

I have attempted to argue elsewhere that railway promotion during the 1830s and early 1840s had an underlying rationality: that its pattern can be explained in terms of the logic of the system's expansion, shifts in technology and in costs, and the availability of resources (human as well as financial) for further promotions (Reed 1975, pp.16–31, 271–2). That is not to dispute that railway promotion became caught up in the speculative manias of 1825, 1835–36, and 1844–45, nor that the reaction to these manias was a powerful deterrent to fresh promotion. However, the lead times imposed by the parliamentary processes were such that the peaks in new authorizations in 1836 and 1845 could not have been directly induced by the contemporary stock market 'highs', and this is confirmed by detailed examination of the chronology of individual promotions. Given that railway shares provided the main focus of trading interest during the booms of 1835–36 and 1844–45, it seems more likely that the markets caught and magnified an optimism which already existed among railway promoters, who had looked at the outcome of earlier projects, assessed current material and labour costs in preparing their estimates, and concluded that further projects were viable.

Further support for this conclusion can be found in the timing of the institutional development of the market. The expansion in provincial exchanges came during 1836 and 1844–45, when railway flotations were already running at a high level, rather than at the outset of the upswings in promotion. The railways' involvement in the febrile markets that developed at the height of the booms cannot be denied, but even this was not entirely attributable to the misguided optimism of the mania phase. The state of company law in England before 1844, together with the nature of the parliamentary authorization processes, made railway securities a particularly high risk investment during the earliest stages of a new company's life. As a consequence the market had a clear role in enabling those prepared to bear this risk to realize the capital gains that were their only means of reward. The margin between such 'legitimate' transfers and outright gambling is in any event difficult to define, but it is questionable whether Keynes' distinction between speculation and enterprise can be applied with any precision during this phase in the development of railways. The data necessary to forecast with reasonable accuracy 'the prospective yield of assets over their whole life' (Keynes 1973, p.158) was simply not available at the stage when parliament required a new undertaking to have the bulk of its capital subscribed.

*
* *

In the course of this inevitably superficial survey I have tried to set out some of my thoughts on the processes of railway investment in Britain during the period that began with the authorization of the Stockton & Darlington Railway and ended with the outbreak of war in 1914. Though I have been out of touch with current work in this field for some time, my personal perception is that this area provides a good example of how individual findings can contribute through their aggregation to a broader and more coherent picture of an entire range of related topics. But if my positive view of past research progress is correct, is there still room for more work on such subjects, or will diminishing returns set in?

My feeling is that, even within the areas I have outlined, there is scope for additional research. The nineteenth-century British railway industry was so large and so heterogeneous that generalizations based on what is still a relatively small sample of companies need further testing, even at the most basic level of the sources of capital for individual railways. One can only deplore the official destruction of so many share registers. But these are not the only sources of information about shareholders. In particular, the Regulation of Railways Act, (1868), required companies to prepare address lists of shareholders, and make copies available for purchase on request. If more of these can be identified, in local archives, in commercial and family collections, or even through the book trade, it should be possible to add to our understanding of the patterns of share ownership.

There is also a need to supplement existing information about equity holdings with a more systematic exploration of preference and guaranteed shareholdings, and of the sources of loan capital. Because subscription contracts provide a starting place for the analysis of the sources of ordinary share capital and the investment behaviour of its holders, research has inevitably been biased towards this class of security. Although the importance of other forms of capital is now well appreciated, it would be valuable to have fuller and more systematic data to supplement the largely a priori analysis upon which this appreciation is based.

It would also be illuminating to have further studies comparable with Irving's work on the North Eastern Railway, to explore the impact on individual companies of changes and pressures in the capital market. One aspect is the effect of these pressures on specific investment decisions. How sensitive were companies to the terms on which they could obtain additional capital for individual projects, and how carefully was such investment appraised? If such research proved possible, it should throw further light on the long-running debate about the railways' performance in the closing decades of the Victorian age and during the Edwardian years. On the supply side, was the North Eastern typical in being 'forced into the City' to place its new issues after 1901 (Irving 1975, pp.144–54)? For the weaker companies, there is much still to be known about the variant forms of finance they were forced to adopt, and the markets in which they operated.

Such topics relate primarily to the railways themselves, though there are obvious crossovers to other sectors of the capital market. However, reverting to the wider context, it may be that further examination of the development phase of the British railway system can add still more to the debate about the nature of the relationship between capital formation and economic growth. In particular, the financing of railway development in Britain provides a case study of the recruitment of capital in forms and on a scale that required the creation of additional mechanisms for this purpose. Besides the transport services they provided, how important in the transmission of economic growth to the wider economy was the railways' specific role in extending the means for the mobilization of capital?[3] Are there also particular regional dimensions of this process which warrant further examination?

I began by acknowledging my remoteness from current academic competence in these areas, and I hope that the preceding observations about possible areas for further work will be taken as lay suggestions rather than as prescriptive. Perhaps in conclusion, though, I can take advantage of my detached status to add a final comment.

The nineteenth-century British railway system was the product of an almost unique set of circumstances. The state of development of the British economy was such that private finance could profitably afford to undertake the provision of social overhead capital without the underwriting of government guarantees, land grants, or direct funding which provided the necessary pump priming for railway systems in many other parts of Europe and the wider world. Later commentators were apt to deplore the heritage of over-capitalization with which, it was claimed, this process had burdened the Big Four companies (Kirkaldy and Evans 1924, pp.138–42; Wood and Stamp, 1928 pp.29–31), while individual shareholders in particular companies sometimes had cause to regret the unintended philanthropy of their investments. By and large, however, the signals of private and social gain coincided during the main development phase of the British railway system, and although relatively unfettered capitalism might be an inefficient way of undertaking the provision of strategic

---

[3]   Compare Mitchell (1964), pp.331–3; Hawke (1970), pp.388–92; and Gourvish (1980), p.33.

infrastructure, it is difficult to think of a similar historical achievement on a comparable scale.

But the judgement of posterity can be harsh. The privatization issues of the 1980s have reintroduced the stag and the bull to a wider public, yet we criticize the expectations of investors in a new industry and an infant capital market in an age long before the disciplines of the Financial Services Act. I wonder how many of us can claim to display in our personal investment decisions, whether in housing, in private means of transport, or in securities, the degree of rationality which we seek to project into the past. If there are any objective lessons from history, surely the Channel Tunnel scheme ought not to have been able to attract private funding. However, history probably also teaches us not to be surprised that it did.

Chapter Three

Railway Development and the Role of the State: Reflections on the Victorian and Edwardian Experience

M. W. Kirby

Introduction

The purpose of this chapter is to provide a critical appraisal of the evolution of government policy in relation to Britain's railways, from their infancy to maturity in the heyday of competitive private enterprise, with a view to raising some key issues for further research. For economic historians it is a commonplace that whilst the pre-1914 decades witnessed the consolidation of *laissez faire* in state–industry relations in the industrial economy in general, the First World War inaugurated an era of increasing interpenetration between government and industry. Whilst the predominantly Conservative administrations of the interwar period sought to resist the collectivist trend in order to preserve the institutions and mechanisms of capitalist free enterprise there is ample evidence to suggest that the ideal of *laissez faire* in the peacetime economy was being undermined. Such legislative enactments as the creation of the Central Electricity Board in 1926, and the cartelization of coal and agriculture after 1929 are all indicative of a movement towards a mixed economy which was to come to full fruition after 1945. In this respect the nationalization of public utilities in the later 1940s was outstanding in so far as it can be equated with a substantial movement towards concentration of ownership and control in the British economy, far removed from the free market ethos of the nineteenth century (Tomlinson 1994). Coincidentally, a contradictory strand in industrial policy was inaugurated in the form of a legislative assault on monopoly power. Whilst the Monopolies and Restrictive Practices Commission, founded in 1948, was officially agnostic on the merits and demerits of monopoly and collusion,' the establishment of the Restrictive Practices Court in 1956 signalled the state's new found commitment to the legal enforcement of competition (Mercer 1995).

In retrospect, however, the contradiction between these policy initiatives was more apparent than real. In formal economic terms public utilities such as gas and electricity enjoy the status of natural monopolies in which access to scale economies determines that a single producer can supply the entire market at a lower average total cost of production than can two or more firms. In this context, public ownership was long viewed as the most appropriate means of securing the public interest against the potential abuse of monopoly power, at least until the 1970s when a combination of changing political ideology and heightened concern with efficiency criteria paved the way for the privatization programme of the 1980s and 1990s. Privatization has not, however, resulted in a return to some mythical *status quo ante* in that former public utilites have been made subject to surveillance by regulatory agencies endowed with statutory powers in the determination of tariffs and prices. In other words, defence of the consumer interest in conditions of natural monopoly, whether under public ownership or regulated privatization, can be viewed as complementary to a pro competitive stance elsewhere in the economy.

A continuing preoccupation with the control of monopoly and the maintenance of competitive structures has thus been at the forefront of industrial policy since the 1940s in reaction to the inexorable trend towards concentration in business observable after 1914. It is salutary to remember, however, that these twentieth-century concerns were fully reflected in public debate in the previous century when fierce competition was the order of the day, at least in manufacturing industry. It is well known that the Cambridge economist, Alfred Marshall, in devising the theory of perfect competition in the 1880s (in which all firms in an industry are price takers), was inspired by the structure of the Lancashire cotton industry which contained a multiplicity of small scale, highly competitive family firms and partnerships (Marshall 1919, pp. 602–3). Some business historians, moreover, in generalizing from cotton textiles, have long noted the delayed recruitment of American style professional managerial hierarchies in British industry and have identified the phenomenon of 'corporate lag' as the primary cause of Britain's relative decline as an industrial power after 1900 (Chandler 1990, pp.235–92; Elbaum and Lazonick 1987). The railway sector, however, stands in stark contrast to manufacturing industry both in respect of competitive and managerial structures. Within fifty years of the opening of the Stockton & Darlington Railway in 1825 the railway system was highly concentrated by contemporary standards. In 1874 there were more than 300 companies open for traffic but 39 per cent of the track mileage was owned by the four largest which collectively earned 47 per cent of the gross receipts. The top ten companies, moreover, accounted for nearly 70 per cent of the mileage and well over 70 per cent of receipts.

Although the degree of concentration hardly increased during the next four decades the whole of the period was overlain by the negotiation of working and pooling agreements which, together with other restrictive practices, were calculated to restrain competitive forces. There were, in addition, three further characteristic features of the railway system which differentiated it from the generality of industry in Victorian and Edwardian Britain. In the first instance, the capitalizations of the dominant companies were huge. On the eve of the First World War, when only a handful of manufacturing firms were capitalized at more than £10 million, each of the nine largest railway companies possessed total paid up capital stocks in excess of £50 million. Secondly, the giants of the industry were themselves the products of innumerable acquisitions and mergers. For example, the GWR, capitalized at £99 million in 1912, was composed of 115 separate undertakings reflecting successive bursts of amalgamation from the 1840s onwards. Indeed, by 1906, 223 of the 351 companies in existence in 1881 had disappeared, mainly as a result of absorption by larger companies. Finally, the railway sector stands apart on account on the managerial structures adopted by the larger companies. As Dr Gourvish has shown, the process of managerial innovation in favour of the recruitment of professional salaried managers differentiated by function, began as early as the 1840s when a number of newly amalgamated undertakings encountered novel problems of large scale control and coordination. New accounting techniques and statistical procedures diffused rapidly thereafter so that by 1900 the railway sector in its corporate guise was matched only by the larger joint stock banking concerns in its commitment to managerial hierarchies (Gourvish 1972).

As a notable island of giantism within a generally disintegrated business structure the railway sector could not fail to attract public interest and discussion. In this respect it is possible to offer an interpretation of state intervention in the industry's affairs which is entirely consistent with the conventional administrative history of the nineteenth century (Taylor 1972, pp. 32–8). The railways, like manufacturing industry and mining, were made subject to safety legislation in the light of operating experience: hardly surprising in the view of the potential for fatalities offered by the new transport medium. By the end of the nineteenth century the conduct of labour relations was on the political agenda: again a predictable development in view of the commercial disruption and substantial personal inconvenience which could follow in the wake of industrial strife. The railways were thus little different to the coalmining industry which also had the potential, via strike action and employers' lockouts, to disrupt the working of the economy as a whole. In two crucial respects, however, the railway sector was treated exceptionally – although hardly consistently – from an early stage of its development, first in the matter of competitive structures and secondly in relation to charges for items of freight. The common denominator between the two issues was the early appreciation by critics of the industry of its inherent structural tendency towards natural monopoly reinforced by the potential for consumer exploitation. In this light the body of this chapter will examine first the evolving competitive structure of the railway industry and the associated reaction of government as a prelude to discussion of government policy with respect to railway charges. The key issues to be highlighted are the apparent inconsistencies in the attitude of the state towards increased concentration and the extent to which increasingly restrictive controls on charging damaged the commercial prospects of the railway companies.

The State and Industrial Structure, 1840-1870

By the end of 1844, of the 104 railway companies then in existence, only 11 possessed lines in excess of fifty miles in total length, with only 11 accounting for more than half of the total route mileage laid down. The early years of British railway development, therefore, had resulted in the proliferation of small undertakings, reflecting parliament's commitment to competitive free enterprise. It was the mid 1840s, however, which witnessed the beginnings of an amalgamation movement which was to characterize the structural evolution of the railway industry, albeit intermittently, down to 1914. A major precipitating factor was the effective management of through traffic necessitating cooperation between adjacent companies. This was facilitated at a relatively early stage by the establishment of the London based Railway Clearing House in 1842. Initially restricted to nine companies, by the end of the decade, in advance of its legal authorization in 1850, it embraced most of the larger undertakings then in existence save for some notable exceptions in the south of England. It is a point well taken that although the organisation 'aimed at removing one of the penalties of dispersed control of railway operations [it] probably tended in practice to demonstrate some of the advantages which amalgamations would bring, and it is arguable that its very existence hastened the process for which it had been designed as an alternative' (Dyos and Aldcroft 1974, p.138).

There is, of course, a human dimension to the company promotions and amalgamations of these years focusing on the person of the York draper and financier, George Hudson. Castigated at the time of his fall from grace in 1849 as a fraudulent and ill bred bounder, Hudson's contribution to the founding of a tolerably rational railway system was invaluable. Promoting only new lines which had a genuine commercial rationale, as a pioneer of amalgamations he succeeded in producing an element of coordinated control over the emergent railway network of eastern England, from London to the Scottish border. This fact in itself encouraged more economical working of the system and helped to improve managerial standards. Responsible for the first great amalgamation of railway undertakings – that of the Birmingham & Derby Junction, Midland Counties & North Midland Railways in 1844 – to form the new Midland Railway (MR), Hudson laid down the groundwork for the subsequent creation of the Great Eastern and North Eastern Railways, the latter enjoying the most complete territorial monopoly of any railway undertaking after its formation in 1854.

Other significant amalgamation schemes of the 1840s included the formation of the Lancashire & Yorkshire Railway (L&YR) after the merger of six separate undertakings in 1845, and the Manchester, Sheffield & Lincolnshire Railway, the product of a four company merger in 1846. But the most impressive amalgamation scheme of these years was the formation in 1846 of the London & North Western Railway (LNWR) following the merger of the trunk line London & Birmingham and Grand Junction Railways. Five years later the new concern was capitalized at more than £29 million, employed a workforce in excess of 12,000 and operated more than 800 miles of track. By that time the LNWR, under its first and most influential general manager, Captain Mark Huish, was at the forefront of managerial innovation embracing accounting procedures which made appropriate allowances for depreciation and plant valuation (especially important given the heavy fixed costs inherent in railway operations) and extensive collection of operating statistics, thereby facilitating the continuous revision of long term costs and an element of forward planning. The board of directors, meeting monthly, was presented with detailed information on costs, augmented where necessary by working papers from senior managers, a number of which in Huish's case represented path-breaking contributions to the theory and practice of railway management (Gourvish 1972, pp.262–5).

There can be little doubt that amalgamations were conducive to the more economical working of the railway system in terms of the handling of through traffic, all the more so since the larger companies, following the lead of the LNWR, succeeded in devising effective managerial structures. But the drive to inceased concentration was propelled also by other inexcapable considerations of economic expediency. In a situation where capital was irredeemable, and where fixed costs were the preponderant element in total costs, any reduction in traffic between competing companies was bound to raise short run unit costs unless competition resulted in an increase in total traffic. As an authoritative commentary has concluded, however, demand for transport services beyond a certain point becomes inelastic with the result that intensified competition would merely raise unit costs to the detriment of net revenure (Dyos and Aldcroft 1974, p.172). Amalgamations, moreover, economized on administrative and managerial expenses, eliminated duplication of facilities and also carriage by circuitous routes, as well as competitive canvassing. It was these considerations which propelled the amalgamation process after 1850 with a further surge in the 1860s. In the latter decade 187 acts of parliament providing for amalgamations reached the statute book. Notable fusions resulted in the formation of the Great Eastern Railway in 1862, the addition of 400 miles to the Great Western Railway system and a 600 mile extension to the route mileage of the LNWR. Further economies of unification were sought via working and leasing agreements which provided for running powers as well as the pooling of receipts and the calculation of common rates of carriage. Indeed, in the early 1860s the number of parliamentary bills providing for such agreements was never less than 40 per annum.

Whilst the economics of railway operations pointed strongly in favour of unification, parliamentary and public reaction to the demonstrable trend towards concentration ebbed and flowed between outright hostility on the one hand and apparent endorsement on the other. It is well known that the first public assault on the railway companies for their monopolistic tendencies was launched as early as 1836 by James Morrison, MP for Ipswich. Taking his stand on the accusation that acts of incorporation for railway companies were tantamount to the endowment of monopoly power, Morrison argued in favour of dividend limitation by statute together with official scrutiny of rates and charges in each twenty-one year period following incorporation. Although Morrison's parliamentary bill was rejected it was only eight years later that W.E. Gladstone, President of the Board of Trade in Peel's administration, took the seemingly radical step of legislating for reduced charges applicable to any company paying dividends in excess of 10 per cent in three consecutive years, together with a provision for state purchase of railways after a period of twenty-one years following parliamentary authorization. Much modified in debate, Gladstone's Regulation of Railways Bill was emasculated: its conditions were not retrospective and therefore rendered pointless the notion of future nationalization. In addition, 10 per cent dividends, with few exceptions, were soon to disappear thereby justifying Clapham's judgement that the purchase and revision clauses of the resulting act were effectively redundant (Barker and Savage 1975, p.75).

Elsewhere, parliamentary intervention in railway affairs at this time was distinctly uneven in its effect. Legislation in 1840 and 1842, for example, empowered the Board of Trade to inspect railways from the standpoint of public safety. In 1844, moreover, Gladstone presided over the formation of a Railway Department at the Board of Trade, charged with the task of scrutinizing railway bills and reporting on them to parliament. The department, however, proved ineffective, as did the succeeding Railway Commission founded in 1846. Whilst the latter survived until 1851 it was, in effect bypassed by parliament's continuing commitment to private bill committees in the matter of railway promotion. In terms of state intervention, therefore, the only noteworthy feature of the 1840s was the clause in Gladstone's Regulation Act of 1844 providing for the 'parliamentary fare' of one penny per mile for third class passengers on a single daily train running throughout the length of a company's line. In other words, the legislative record of the 1840s failed to reflect emergent public and parliamentary concerns with the potential abuse of monopoly power. In this setting the railways were indeed enjoying a 'legal honeymoon' before 1850, a honeymoon, moreover, which was to continue down to the early 1870s when a new constellation of political forces, reinforced by changing economic circumstances, resulted in an increasingly interventionist stance on the part of both Liberal and Conservative administrations (Dyos and Aldcroft 1974, p.142).

In accounting for parliament's quiescence in relation to the marked trend towards concentration observable from the later 1840s onwards, Henry Parris in a seminal study has observed that the period to 1867 was characterized by a temporary diminuation in party loyalties which enabled members of both Houses with railway interests to combine together to oppose interventionist legislation. There was, in effect, an overriding 'Railway Interest' which encouraged parliamentarians of differing political allegiances to incur the displeasure of their nominal party leaders with impunity (Parris 1965, p.213). The apparent influence of the the 'Railway Interest' was well illustrated in the findings of the Select Committee on Railway Amalgamations which reported in 1872. Appointed to deliberate on the implications for rail users of a flurry of bills for amalgamations and working agreements in the 1870s, including the proposed fusion of the LNWR and L&YR, the committee concluded in a famous judgement that in the face of the trend towards concentration observable in the previous 25 years it was evident that, 'Competition must fail to do for the railways what it has done for ordinary trade and that no means have yet been devised by which competition can be permanently maintained' (cited in Dyos and Aldcroft 1974, p.164).

In viewing amalgamations as both inevitable and desirable the Select Committee commented that 'the balance of advantage to the public as well as to the shareholders, may after all be thought to be on the side of amalgamation', a judgement validated by the commercial practices of the NER, a company enjoying a territorial monopoly but which combined the lowest fares and charges with the highest dividend record of any English railway since its inception in 1854. But despite an acceptance of the logic of amalgamations the committee was concerned to encourage the more effective scrutiny of the commercial practices of railway companies. In this respect it referred back to the Railway and Canal Traffic Act of 1854, itself the product of earlier select committee deliberations, which had sought to define key principles of commercial practice under monopoly conditions. These included a requirement that terms and conditions of carriage should be 'reasonable', that 'undue or unreasonable preference' should be outlawed, and that 'all due and reasonable facilities' should be offered to traffic senders 'without unreasonable delay'. The body responsible for implementing these requirements – the Court of Common Pleas – had proved ineffective; and in noting this fact the later Select Committee proposed the establishment of a small but expert Railway Commission charged with the task not only of examining all future proposals for amalgamation and working agreements with veto powers in the public interest, but also of implementing the provisions of the act of 1854 more effectively. These recommendations were enacted under the Railway and Canal Traffic Act of 1873.

Historians of public policy in relation to the railways are agreed that the act of 1873 marked the onset of a 'new era' in the history of state intervention, particularly in relation to charging policy (Dyos and Aldcroft 1974, p.166). As the following section will indicate, this was the product of changing political and economic relationships which were to reach their climax in the enforced amalgamation of railway companies in the aftermath of the First World War. Before examining the later Victorian and Edwardian experience, however, it is appropriate to offer considered judgement on the evolution of government policy in the formative years of railway development up to 1870.

One of the most striking features of the early development of Britain's railways was the early appreciation by both rail users and parliamentarians of their potential for monopolistic abuse. To the extent that the overwhelming majority of railway companies derived their powers from parliamentary acts, they were effectively 'the creatures of parliament' (Parris 1965, p.18). It was this perspective on state–industry relations which informed Morrison's strictures in 1836, closely followed by the appointment of a select committee in 1839 which focused attention for the first time on the distinctive nature of railway economics. As the committee observed, the original intentions of parliament in giving legal authorization to railway companies was that free competition would be guaranteed by the presence of independent carriers paying tolls to the sponsoring railway company. The practicalities of railway operations, however, demanded 'one system of management entailing monopolistic control' (Parris 1965, p.9). Contemporary Benthamite and *laissez-faire* doctrines allowed for state regulation in order to preempt irresponsible monopolistic authority. The succeeding legislative record, however, from the formation of the Railway Department of the Board of Trade in 1844, through the Railway Board and the Railway Commission of the later 1840s, and the reincarnation of the Department in 1851, was marked by vacillation and uncertainty. Concerns were expressed about railway safety as well as wages and hours of work of railway personnel. Gladstone's doctrine of 'equivalents', moreover, held out the prospect of reconciling moves towards concentration with lower rates and fares. In overall terms, however, the lack of a consistent policy was reflected in the continuing commitment of parliament to the system of private bill committees. The result, in the context of the mania of company speculation in the later 1840s, was that the embryonic railway system reached early maturity with little or no government regulation. Nevertheless, the emergent rail network was hardly anarchic. Hudson's role as a sponsor of rational amalgamations was outstanding. The foundation of the Railway Clearing House facilitated through traffic and enabled accounts to be kept and balances to and from each company to be settled. By 1853, sixty-five companies were members, including all those of importance except for the GWR, which was excluded because of its broad gauge. The associated company conferences in bringing separate railway management together, facilitated close cooperation and in all likelihood encouraged further concentration. Above all, perhaps, the larger companies in the period to 1870 made major strides towards resolving the problems of large-scale managerial control. Pioneered by the LNWR, organisational and financial innovations, devised and implemented by a new class of professional, salaried managers, rebounded to the advantage of the system as a whole by improving overall efficiency.

The State and the Regulation of Charges, 1873-1914

While the middle decades of the nineteenth century had witnessed a substantial movement towards concentration of railway companies it is notable that from the 1870s onwards the rate of amalgamation fell off significantly. Mergers continued to take place, but in general they reflected the absorption of small, short lines by neighbouring larger companies. In accounting for the slackening trend towards amalgamation railway historians have identified two complementary factors. In the first instance, the fact of substantial concentration by 1870 served in itself to restrict the opportunities for further large amalgamations. Secondly, the period after 1870 witnessed greater parliamentary and rail user hostility to amalgamations, well illustrated in the early 1870s by the failure of the proposed merger of the Midland and Glasgow & South Western Railways, and of the LNWR and L&YR (Cain 1988, p.118). Amalgamations on this scale would have led to significant increases in the level of concentration and in both instances parliament acted decisively to reject them in the face of rail users' fears of monopolization. In this respect, Parris has offered the apposite judgement that as the franchise spread in the wake of the 1867 Reform Act, 'the number interested in lower rail charges came to exceed the number of those interested in high profits' (Parris 1965, p.214). Within parliament itself the power of parties was growing in the final quarter of the nineteenth century and with MPs increasingly dependent on their constituencies, the power of vested interests – well represented in the 'Railway Interest' – began to decline.

In the context of an increasingly adverse political climate the railway companies were thus obliged to seek alternative means of restricting competition. As noted already, collusive activity was well established before 1870 in the form of working and pooling agreements and conferences for agreeing rates. These practices, however, become even more apparent after

1870, all the more so since their implementation did not require parliamentary approval. In structural terms the net effect of this trend was to produce, by the turn of the century, a railway system subject to 'collusive oligopoly' in respect of price and certain aspects of qualifying service (Dyos and Aldcroft 1974, p.170). But although qualified 'competition among the few' is an acceptable generalization for the system as a whole, monopolistic and duopolistic elements were strongly represented in specific geographical areas, in the north-east of England, for example, and parts of the south-west. It is therefore paradoxical at first sight that in the face of these structural trends, competitive processes remained stubbornly alive after 1870. External competition, for example, was sustained down to the outbreak of the First World War when motor vehicles were first beginning to supplement electric tramways in making inroads into the urban short distance traffic of the railways. In the 1870s and 1880s canals were still an important alternative transport medium in the West Riding and South Lancashire. Even more significant as a constraint on railway monopoly was coastal shipping, hardly surprising in a country where most large urban concentrations had easy access to ports and where the business of importing and exporting was such a vital part of the commercial infrastructure. The North Eastern Railway, in particular, was vulnerable to competition from this source and also from 'the competition of districts'. As the first historian of the company observed, the NER was bound to maintain competitive rates and facilities if only to sustain the competitiveness of major industrial traffic senders both at home and abroad (Tomlinson 1915, reprint 1967, pp.5–11). The NER directorate, moreover, was composed of interlocking industrial interests and as the company's most recent historian has concluded, 'the North Eastern [Railway] might be regarded as a sort of holding company for the region as a whole' and to that extent its pricing policy may have been calculated 'to maximize not just company profit but to some extent also the profit of local industry' (Irving 1976, p.38).

If traffic senders could take comfort from these checks on monopoly power they also stood to gain from collusion itself. Working agreements, like amalgamations, helped reduce or eliminate conveyance by circuitous routes, thereby curtailing delivery costs and facilitating more economical working via fuller loading. An outstanding example of the economic advantages of collusion is provided by the working agreement between the MR and the LNWR which saved the former 3,000 train miles per week in carrying meat between London and Carlisle.

A further source of advantage for the trading community in the later nineteenth century was provided by substantial improvements in the quality of railway services. The most obvious manifestations of this were on the passenger side where improved standards of comfort for third class passengers were complemented by reduced journey times, a greater emphasis on safety and a permanent way of higher quality as wrought iron rails were replaced by steel. For traders the main advances took the form of branch line extensions, the construction of major tunnels and bridges, and duplication of the permanent way subject to heavy use. Altogether, the total route mileage was increased from over 13,500 in 1870 to about 18,000 in 1895, a period which also witnessed the demise of the Great Western's broad gauge (Barker and Savage 1975, p.97).

In the light of these advances in service provision, and against a background of continuing competition even in the context of collusion, it might be thought that traffic senders would be content with their lot. This was far from the case. Indeed, the later nineteenth century is notable for a rising tide of complaint from the trading community which, in concert with the changing political environment referred to above, was to lead to substantial measures of state intervention. The economic context for these developments was provided by the onset of foreign competition, first in the domestic grain market, spreading then to the import of frozen meat, and from the later 1880s reflected in a rising tide of manufactured imports from Germany and the USA. Indeed, the years 1873–96 were designated at the time as the 'Great Depression' in trade and industry denoting a sustained period of deflation and falling profit margins.

Although economic historians have emphasized the continuing increase both in total output and real incomes throughout this period, there can be little doubt that the trading community, in seeking to reduce costs, focused its attention in part on railway traffic charges. In one sense traders were right to do so, in that railway rates were falling less rapidly than the general price index after 1873, so that the real cost of transport was rising in late Victorian Britain. Orchestrated by numerous Chambers of Commerce, traders also claimed that rail charges were higher in Britain than in the USA, and they were in no way placated by the response of the railway companies that the norm of shorter journeys and smaller loads in Britain was bound to be reflected in higher charges than in a country of continental proportions. Above all, however, the companies were accused of unfair discrimination in their charges. As Cain has emphasized, the Railway and Canal Traffic Act of 1854 allowed companies to discriminate only on the basis of costs, whereas by the 1880s their pricing decisions were being determined primarily by reference to competition with shipping companies. Inland manufacturers, therefore, were loud in their complaints that they were being penalized in favour of competitors with port locations (Cain 1988, p.107). A further issue of extreme sensitivity related to the habit the companies had of carrying goods from a port of arrival at rates lower than those charged to home producers using only part of the same route. Again, their defence that this was part of the normal competitive process in the railway system – since failure to offer preferential rates would merely divert trade to another port to the advantage of the railway which served it – was less than acceptable to hard pressed traders.

Against this background of mounting dissatisfaction on the part of rail users and increasingly defensive railway companies, parliament acted in the later 1880s to impose a uniform classification and maximum charging schedules over the entire railway network in Great Britain. Select Committees had already deliberated in 1881 and 1882 on complaints relating to excessive charges, but although the companies were absolved of 'grave dereliction of their duties to the public', and it was accepted that differential charges were not necessarily against the public interest, the relevant reports registered significant dissatisfaction with the multiplicity of rates and charges across the system. With 2,753 identifiable commodities in 1886 according to the Railway Clearing House classification, together with 18,000 railway stations, the number of separate rates was enormous: in excess of 13 million on the Great Northern and 20 million on the LNWR. Thus, the Railway and Canal Traffic Act, passed by a Conservative government in 1888, provided for a detailed review of maximum charges in Great Britain. It also established the Railway and Canal Commission (the renamed Railway Commission) as a judicial surveillance body and gave to a commission appointed by the Board of Trade the task of devising both a revised schedule of charges and a new classification for merchandise. Whilst the latter proved to be uncontroversial, the fixing of new maximum rates was to lead to a renewed outbreak of hostility against the railway companies.

After prolonged negotiation a new charging scheme was to come into operation on 1 January 1893. Although the new rates had been calculated simply on the basis of existing charges, the railway companies were made subject to more explicit criteria for the outlawing of undue preference and discrimination in favour of foreign merchandise. The main innovation, however, was the introduction of tapering charges by which rates per mile diminished as distance increased, thereby establishing for the first time the principle that rates charged should be related to operating costs. When the new rates were introduced, however, traders found that while some had been lowered, others had been raised to the new maximum without explanation. Whether this was the product of company greed or bureaucratic confusion is immaterial since the eventual outcome was a further Railway and Canal Traffic Act, passed in 1894, which gave the Railway and Canal Commissioners the power to restrict charges to the levels of 1892.

The legislation of 1888 and 1894 represented a further important milestone in the history of state intervention in the railway sector. In imposing new and unprecedented rigidities in charging policies it confronted the railway companies with vital questions of future strategy, especially in a general context of increasingly expensive non-price competition and when operating costs were on a rising trajectory. In the latter context the reversal of the general price fall after 1896 entailed a substantial rise in material costs at the very time when labour costs were being inflated by restrictive legislation on hours of work. Confronted by declining profitability in the face of high and rising operating costs, some of the larger railway companies responded with a mixture of internal reforms, buttressed by a new drive towards cooperation after 1900. The NER for example, borrowing from North American precedents, introduced new management procedures leading to more effective monitoring of operating costs. Elsewhere, capital expenditure programmes were trimmed and unprofitable facilities withdrawn at the same time as pooling arrangements proliferated (Cain 1988, pp.109–17). Above all, the period gave rise to a new drive towards amalgamation in order to achieve scale economies in the pursuit of higher profitability. This movement reached its peak between 1906 and 1910 when ambitious proposals for a full working union (i.e., merger falling short of combining the respective capital stocks) were advanced by the Great Central, Great Northern and Great Eastern Railways. Less ambitious schemes for union were subsequently advanced by the LNWR, and the Lancashire and Yorkshire and Midland Railways. The movement was replicated in Scotland and also in the increased cooperation observable between the Great Western and London & South Western Railways after 1910.

Predictably, such overt moves in favour of increased concentration, involving several of the largest railway undertakings then in existence, did not go unchallenged. Although the 'Greats' scheme of 1907 had the backing of the Board of Trade, a bill to effect it only nominally passed its second reading in 1909, despite the fact that the companies were required to maintain their pre-merger facilities. The companies thereupon withdrew their bill, but agreed to participate in a departmental committe of enquiry established by the Board of Trade to investigate the likely problems to be raised by further combination. In one sense the resulting report represented a major advance in official thinking on the organisation of railways in that it accepted 'the growth of cooperation and the more complete elimination of competition as a process at once inevitable and likely to be beneficial both to the railway companies themselves, and if properly safeguarded, to the public also' (Cain 1972, pp.623–6). A bill to give effect to the recommendations of the committee in the form of a 'code of practice' for state regulation of combinations was introduced in 1912, but hastily withdrawn in the face of entrenched opposition both within and without parliament. Quite apart from the continuing and unremitting hostility of traders to the spectre of monopolistic abuse, the timing was unpropitious in that it followed on immediately after a national railway strike. The response of the government had been to pressurize the railway companies into offering more generous conditions and pay, a policy which carried with it the implicit assumption that charges would be raised. This was achieved under the Railway and Canal Traffic Act of 1913 but the damage had been done: governmental support for increased concentration, even when buttressed by the prospect of further regulatory authorities, was deeply unpopular even though, ironically, it was traders' insistence on an unsupportable degree of non-price competition which had produced the new impetus towards combination. In the event, the Liberal Government reverted to that classic British device for reconciling the irreconcilable: the appointment of a Royal Commission in 1914 to investigate the future organisation of railways, including the prospects for public ownership. Its deliberations ceased, however, on the outbreak of war in August 1914.

Conclusion

In surveying the structural evolution of Britain's railway system before 1914 it is impossible not to be impressed by the logical inevitability of increased concentration. To contemporary observers both within and without parliament this was not so much the result of the practical economics of railway operations, consistent with the interests of the generality of rail users, but of the drive towards monopoly and its inevitable concomitant: the exploitation of consumers. At times there were signs of official recognition of the economics of unification; as reflected in the Select Committe reports of 1872 and 1912; but governments in general sought either to sustain the market force of competition or to regulate rail charges. In doing so they were responding to the clamour of rail users and an increasingly effective pro-competition lobby at Westminster as the 'Railway Interest' declined in numbers and influence after 1870. Yet the history of state intervention demonstrates all too clearly that parliament, in responding to the clamour, succeeded in pursuing at one and the same time the economically incompatible principles of monopoly and competition. To that extent the railway companies were subject to profound inconsistencies in state policy. Nowhere was this more apparent than in the aftermath of the 1894 Railway and Canal Traffic Act which, in drastically reducing flexibility in charging policy, propelled the railway companies down the route of increasingly costly non-price competition which resulted ultimately in a renewed drive towards concentration after 1906. In this respect attempts by parliament to satisfy the perceived needs of rail users produced a response from the railway companies that was equally repugnant to rail users. It is hardly surprising, therefore, that after 1890 the companies felt that they were being pressed to take on a public utility role wholly inconsistent with their status as commercial undertakings responsible, first and foremost, to their shareholders.

In identifying a research agenda for economic historians interested in relations between government and industry in the early railway sector, the key issue for debate must be the extent to which the operating efficiency and profitability of the railway companies was adversely affected by the ambiguities and inconsistencies of government policy. This was especially the case in relation to the continuing public and parliamentary scepticism concerning the economic benefits to be derived from further concentration via company amalgamations. Recent work by Foreman-Peck has pointed to the positive efficiency gains to be obtained from greater concentration in an industry subject to high fixed costs and sustained user pressure for uneconomic service provision. In that light, a more relaxed public stance with regard to mergers could well have rebounded to the advantage, not just of the railway companies, but also to the economy as a whole in terms of the reduced cost of transport provision. Yet in the current state of knowledge a credible counterfactual analysis of the economic gains to be derived from increased concentration does not exist. The fact remains that the pre-1914 railway system was subject to a variety of influences which retarded efficiency so that the calculation of the gains from further concentration would need to be offset by detailed analysis of a much wider constellation of factors in which the historical present was determined in large measure by the legacy of the past.

In relation to access to managerial economies of scale, reference has been made to the role of the larger railway companies as pioneers of corporate forms of organisation staffed by professional salaried managers differentiated by function. But as Foreman-Peck has emphasized, it was the managerial cadres of the late nineteenth and early twentieth centuries which set their face against the collection of ton mile and passenger mile statistics which would have pointed the way towards increased efficiency arising from heavier train loading (Foreman-Peck and Millward 1994, p.6). With few exceptions, moreover, the railway companies permitted the survival of low productivity working practices with the result that advances in labour productivity lagged far behind North American achievements. Above all, the response to mounting cost pressures after 1880 was to squeeze wages and lengthen hours of work to the detriment of safety and the quality of labour relations.

Such a conservative response may well have been intensified by an increasingly introspective generation of managers recruited from within the railway sector rather than from outside as in the period to 1870, thereby rendering the industry less receptive to innovation (Foreman-Peck and Millward 1994, pp.90–1). In this setting, the economic history of the early railway sector, in so far as it pertains to the role of the state, is far from complete; there is a considerable volume of high quality literature on cognate parts of the industry's history, but what is lacking is an all embracing view of the achievements and limitations of offical policy in practice. This is a necessary prerequisite for greater understanding of the counterfactual possibilities inherent in an expanded role for the state in the period in question.

Chapter Four

The Historical Geographer's Approach to Railway History: The Relations between Railways and Canals

D. Turnock

Historical geographers have always paid close attention to transport networks (Carter 1959; Fullerton 1975) and their studies of spatial relationships over the last two centuries have inevitably brought railways to the fore (Freeman and Aldcroft 1985; 1988). A popular approach has been to consider the engineering work necessary to cope with varying topographical conditions and the decision-making involved in selecting railway routes through challenging terrain (Appleton 1962; O'Dell 1956; O'Dell and Richards 1971). This could be linked with aesthetic issues concerning the impact of the railway in different landscape settings, including the perceptions of damage to scenery arising from the intrusion of railways into sensitive areas. The networks of individual railway companies and their relations with each other have also been investigated for Britain, Germany and the former USSR by R.E.H. Mellor (1969; 1979; 1995). Geographical approaches have also considered the socio-economic landscape in order to highlight the impact of the railways on various aspects of economy and society (Turnock 1990; 1998). The epic work of J.R. Kellett (1969) on the significance of railways for the organisation of cities is paralleled by geographical studies of urban networks (Patmore 1964) and a growing number of papers which examine the links between industry and transport in specific local contexts (Chandler 1957; Siviour 1974). But there is also the question of competition between different transport modes. How did the railways find a niche in a transport system dominated in the early nineteenth century by roads and navigations; and how did the expansion of the railway system impact on their competitors? This is the thrust of the present paper which gives particular attention to the fate of the canals during the 'Railway Age', including the ownership of canals by railway companies and the scope for competition between canal and railway interests in the later part of the nineteenth century.

Roads and Canals at the Dawn of the Steam Railway Era

The development of the steam railways followed a half century which saw 'no fundamental revolution in transport technology [for] what essentially prevailed was a constant process of adjustment and improvement to preexisting transport technologies' (Freeman 1988, p.16). 'Road, water and wagonway transport appear to have been servicing the needs of the industrializing economy without undue difficulty' and the transformation of railway potentials by the steam locomotive must certainly have seemed most bothersome to those who were satisfied with a steady pace of innovation that would not disturb the established order (Freeman 1988, p.16). Vested interests in other sectors of the transport business were particularly troubled and none more than the turnpike trusts and road users. Although there were experiments with the steam coach on the roads (notably by Walter Hancock in 1833), there was hostility from the turnpike trusts, which imposed heavy tolls. This helped to ensure that the locomotive would be kept off the highways and 'confined to its own particular right of way, properly fenced in, though it was not until 1835 that parliament dealt with this matter in the Highways Act of that year' (Sherrington 1934, p.41). While it must remain doubtful whether a more accommodating attitude by the turnpike trusts could have brought steam traction on to the roads, to the mutual advantage of the operators and road managers, there is no doubt that railways quickly eliminated competition from horse drawn coaches and wagons (Barker 1986; Spencer 1977). They were displaced to the feeder routes on which the country carrier continued to flourish for the rest of the century (Everitt 1976; Turnbull 1969), acting as 'a kind of primitive country bus, often a mere cart, conveying the village folk (especially women and children) to the local town on market day.' (Everitt 1973, pp.217–19).

The position of the waterways is rather more complicated. Initially, they provided a major stimulus for railway development. The wagonway offered a cost-effective technology which linked navigations to mineral sources that were too awkwardly situated for a conventional solution to be feasible (Baxter 1966). As the coalmasters of Durham and Northumberland strove to increase efficiency on their wagonways at the turn of the eighteenth century, their economic power hastened the perfection of the steam locomotive. The railway could also be used as a bridge between waterways, passing through difficult terrain with differences in level that would otherwise have required complex lockage, as in the case of the Charnwood Forest Canal's railway between the canal at Nanpantan (275 feet) and the navigable Soar in Loughborough (150 feet), or the line built by the Lancaster Canal to connect the Walton level at 275 feet with the Ribble Valley just above sea level (Hadfield and Biddle 1979). Sometimes such railways were temporary, as in the case of the line from Blisworth to Stoke Bruerne (1800–5) which was intended as a stop gap pending completion of Blisworth Tunnel, or the railway from Gayton at 300 feet to Northampton at 190 feet (1805–15), which was superseded by a conventional canal as a condition for the construction of the Grand Union Canal (GUC) (Faulkner 1972; Hatley 1970). Many of these railways have disappeared but a proportion were eventually modernized for locomotive running, becoming part of the public network, and some continue to be used like Dow Low Quarry branch south of Buxton which comprises a modernized section of the Cromford & High Peak Railway of 1833, built to connect the Cromford and Peak Forest canals across the Peak District (Hodgkiss 1978; Marshall 1982; Rimmer 1985).

Railways were not regarded as serious rivals until lines were built to duplicate canals, like the L&M or the Glasgow & Garnkirk: soon to be followed by much larger projects like the LBR in England or the Edinburgh & Glasgow Railway in Scotland, completed in 1838 and 1842 respectively. In Ireland, where the initial expectation had been state encouragement and assistance for a coordinated canal-rail transport system, the Dublin–Galway line which ran parallel to the Royal Canal as far as Mullingar was completed in 1851. The opposition mounted by canal companies was ineffective in the face of a parliament determined to prevent vested interests stifling the development of the railway system (Bagwell 1988). After they had 'first scoffed at the railways as "nothing more than insane schemes" or as costly "bubbles"..., they reduced their tolls and they also considered how they could improve their canals' (Pratt 1912, p.296). This was by no means easy, for not only did the reduction in tolls mean that less money was available for development, but the system as a whole was difficult to modernize. In the opinion of Nicholas Wood, author of a *Practical Treatise on Rail-Roads*, the nature of canals 'almost prohibits the application of mechanical power to advantage in the conveyance of goods and passengers' (Pratt 1912, p.297). There was an obvious problem through the frequent interruptions to a journey by locks (all the greater when barge trains were used) while the threat to canal banks through wash limited the speed of boats once mechanical power became available. Lack of standardization inhibited long voyages by boats working at full capacity, while the dimensions of the locks limited the size of boat that could be used.

Improvements were therefore geared to better all year round availability through more adequate water supply (against summer drought) and an improved ice breaking service in winter, while some canals eased the pressure at bottlenecks. Such developments were very necessary and would have been made earlier had the canal companies not exploited their advantages so aggressively. For as R.D. Baxter asserted 'the canal companies enjoyed a virtual monopoly. Their agents were despotic in their treatment of the great houses which supported them...the facilities of transit were manifestly deficient: barges got aground...during summer [and] in severe winters were frozen up for weeks' (Baxter 1866, p.565). It was this 'intolerable tyranny' that helped produce the Liverpool & Manchester Railway (Baxter 1866, p.565). There is perhaps an element of exaggeration because it was not railway competition that led to the removal of Brindley's Smethwick Summit of 1769 by Smeeton in 1790, with further improvement by Telford in 1824

(Broadbridge 1974). And it was the possibility of a new canal project (London & Birmingham Junction) to link Birmingham with the capital (and not the LBR) that pressurized the Oxford Canal into shortening the canal between Hawkesbury and Napton by cutting through a succession of Brindley's contouring meanders; work carried out in 1834 according to surveys by M.I. Brunel in 1828 saved a total of fourteen miles (Boucher 1968; Compton 1976, pp.93–5). But there was no doubt that more needed to be done. Cold winters occurred with greater frequency than today and involved closures for periods of several weeks on end. There was a five week closure on the Trent & Mersey Canal (TMC) in 1814–15 and disruptions which cumulatively amounted to a similar period of closure on the Huddersfield Canal in 1822–23. Summer droughts could also prove disruptive.

On the Oakham Canal the projected reservoir at Langham was never built and the small storage at Oakham was too small to prevent crises in 1804, 1832 and 1836. Despite the diversion of a stream near Ashwell, the canal was shut for five months in 1844 (Tew 1984, pp.64–8). Traders who could not afford such delays were forced to use road transport which was considerably more expensive (Freeman 1983, p.7). However the construction of extra reservoirs (or pumping stations) and the introduction of ice breakers was more straightforward than the replacement of locks by lifts. The technological and financial problems prevented significant progress and canals continued to be handicapped by the repeated interruption of journeys which could arise on average between one and three times each mile (calculated on a company basis). Delays could be increased by queues of boats, a situation that could be relieved by duplicating flights of locks, as at Stoke Bruerne on the Grand Junction Canal (GJC) or at Blackhill on the Monkland Canal where the locks were complemented by an inclined plane between 1850 and 1887. However, there was a programme of lock improvements on the Aire & Calder where a 206 by 22 foot chamber was installed at Pockington in 1860 as the start of a rolling programme which was completed in 1873. Improvements were carried out on the Weaver, first between the 1840s and 1870s and again during the later years of the century when capacity became adequate for 1,000 ton loads; there was also a Mersey entrance lock provided at Weston Point (1856) and a lift at Anderton to link the Weaver with the Bridgewater Canal (1875). Locks were installed for the first time on the Severn between Diglis (near Worcester) and Stourport, with Tewkesbury following in 1858. And by 1888 the Severn was dredged to give a depth of six to nine feet throughout. Improvements on the Trent involving bypass canals with navigation locks were carried out over a long period between 1801 and 1926 (Lewin 1981; Willan 1936; Duncan 1981). Even so, much of the river trade was lost to the railway. At Radcliffe the effect of the Nottingham–Grantham railway was 'to reduce river traffic to insignificance and to obliterate the wharf' (Priestland 1989, p.119). Eight men in the village earned a living on the river in 1851 but there were none at all 30 years later.

A New Environment for Canal Trade

Parliament gave some protection to the waterways and the Oxford, Worcester & Wolverhampton Railway was obliged to compensate the Severn Commissioners when their toll revenue fell below £14,000 per annum. The same company also had to purchase the Stratford-upon-Avon Canal to overcome opposition. In the teeth of threats to build rival railways, the GWR and LNWR were obliged to accommodate the Kennet & Avon and Birmingham Canal Navigations respectively: the former by purchase (with an obligation to continue operation) and the latter by guarantees of a minimum return on capital (Hadfield 1984 p.277; Pratt 1912 pp.297-8).In either case the canals were subsidized to an extent from railway company profits. If the canal was owned by a railway company it had to be kept in repair (and might therefore be promoted to the extent of meeting the costs of its upkeep). Fig 4.1 and Table 4.1 show the situation over railway ownership in 1912. There were twelve companies with waterway interests and in four cases the length was greater than 100 miles: the LNWR with 498, the GWR with 225, the North Staffordshire Railway (NSR) with 119 and the Great Central Railway with 104.

Legislation in 1873 and 1888 laid down safeguards governing railway control of canals. Where canal companies remained they were supported by strong parliamentary backing for an independent existence in competition with the railways. Certainly the legislative environment which parliament created meant that there were situations where the canals maintained a competitive edge. In such cases companies 'were astounded by the fact that, notwithstanding the immense traffic conveyed by rail, their own traffic and receipts continued to increase; and that in common with other interests they fully shared in the expansion of trade and commerce which had been so effectually promoted by the extension of the railway system' (Smiles 1862, pp.280-1). There were regional systems of coal distribution based on the Black Country, Central Lancashire, Forest of Dean and South Yorkshire fields. And some local extensions to the network were made on this basis, like the Cannock Extension and the Wyrley Bank Branch. The same point could be made in respect of the limestone traffic because the NSR initially improved access from Caldon Low to the head of the Caldon Canal at Froghall by replacing the tramroad of 1802 with a more substantial railway in 1849: 'it was cable-operated and of 3 feet 6 inches gauge [with] four self-acting planes' (Lindsay 1979, p.141). Only in 1905 was there a standard gauge link with the Waterhouses line at Caldon Junction leading to the abandonment of the link with the Caldon Canal in 1920. The traffic flows from the ports were thoroughly viable provided major increases in capacity were not required, such as the shipment of pottery materials from the Mersey to North Staffordshire as well as attempts to compete for passenger transport through the operation of fly-boat services. The journey from Liverpool to Manchester could be completed in 16 hours. 'The best fly-boats required only two days between Birmingham and Lancashire, though most took three or four, as

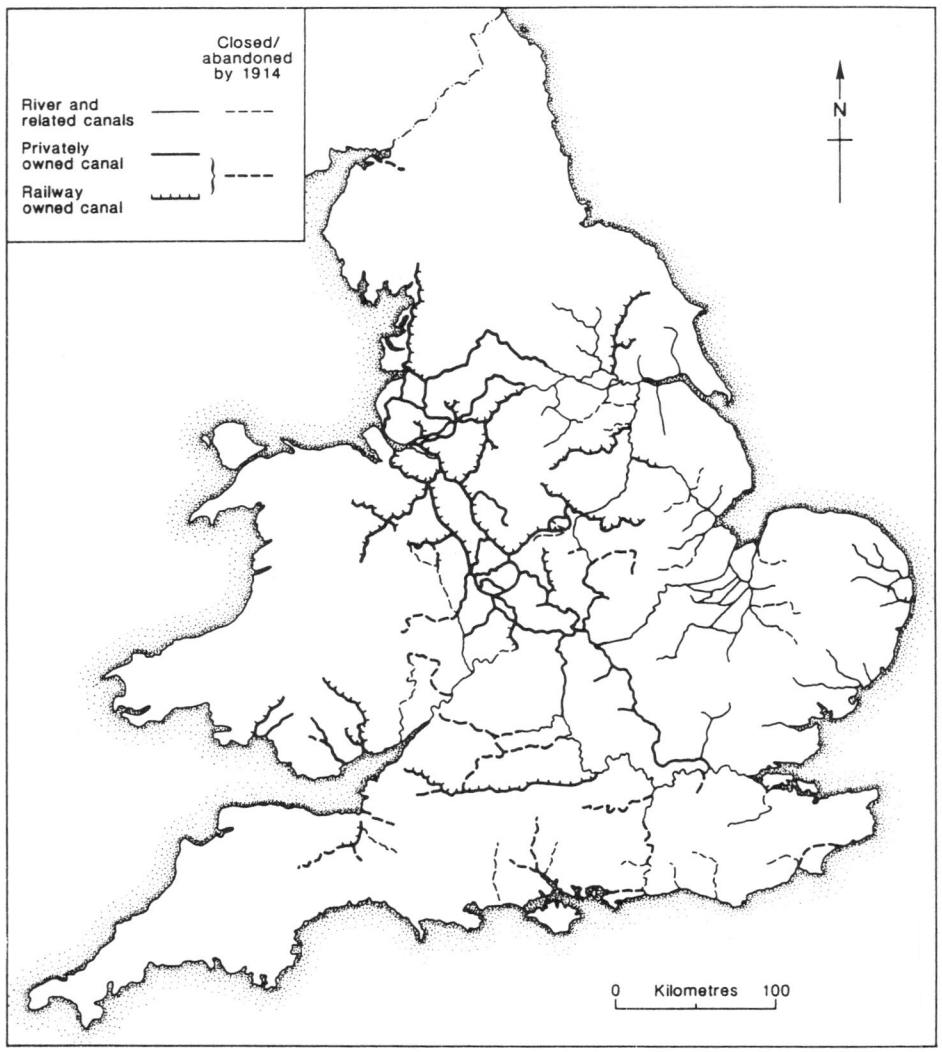

Figure 4.1: Inland waterways under railway ownership in 1912

also did the stage boats from Birmingham to London' (Duckham 1983, p.127).

Table 4.1
Inland waterways owned by railway companies 1912

Railway Company	Waterways Owned	A	B	C	D
Caledonian	Forth & Clyde	1867	40	41	19x66
	Monkland	1867	15	18	13x66
Furness	Ulverston	1862	1	1	17x104
Great Central	Ashton	1848	18	25	7x70
	Chesterfield	1846	45	65	7x72
	Peak Forest	1846	15	16	7x70
	Macclesfield	1846	26	12	7x70
Great Northern	Fossdyke	1846	11	1	15x78
	Grantham	1861	33	18	14x75
	Nottingham	1861	15	19	14x75
	Witham	1846	36	2	15x78
Great Western	Brecknock & Abergavenny	1880	33	6	9x65
	Bridgewater & Taunton	1866	15	7	13x54
	Grand Western	1854	24	10	7x26(a)
	Kennett & Avon	1852	86	106	14x70(b)
	Monmouthshire	1880	20	63	9x65
	Stourbridge	1846	3	1	7x72
	Stover	1862	2	5	14x54
	Stratford		26	56	7x72
	Swansea	1873	16	36	7x69
Lancashire & Yorkshire	Manchester, Bolton & Bury	1847	16	17	14x68
London & North Western	Birmingham Nav	1846	150	203	7x71
	Coalport	1857	1	1	6x20
	Huddersfield	1844	23	51	7x70(c)
	Lancaster	1885	70	20	14x72
	St Helens	1845	16	14	17x68(d)
	Shropshire Union	1847	238	147	7x72
Midland	Ashby	1846	30	0	
	Oakham	1847	15	19	14x72

4.1 concluded

Railway Company	Waterways Owned	A	B	C	D
Midland Great Western	Royal	1846	96	46	13x75
North British	Edinburgh & Glasgow	1865	32	11	12x69
North Eastern	Derwent	1855	39	5	14x55
	Pocklington	1847	21	9	14x57
	Ripon	1845	10	5	14x57
North Staffordshire	Trent & Mersey	1847	119	94	7x72(e)
South Eastern & Chatham	Thames & Medway	1846	7	2	22x94

A Date of acquisition
B Length (miles) including branches
C Number of locks (including locks on branch canals)
D Lock dimensions (feet)
(a) including lifts and inclines
(b) 16x75 on the River Avon
(c) 14x58 on the broad section
(d) 20x75 on the broad section
(e) 13x72 on the broad section

Source : The Railway Yearbook for 1912

Canals also entered into railway company controversies. When the Shrewsbury & Birmingham Railway (SBR) tried to forward traffic to Birmingham along the canal in 1850, at a time when the LNWR was holding up work on the Stour Valley line (the intended means of SBR access to the city), a LNWR party was despatched to disrupt the transfer operations. The SBR were given military protection so that the work could be completed and the company went on to build its own set of wharves (Victoria Basin) (Morriss 1983, p.30). The LNWR were again aware of the significance of canals when they leased the Shropshire Union in 1857 and used the waterway to compete with the Cambrian Railways and the GWR in the Welsh border country (Turnock 1990, p.104). Another example concerns the Grand Canal in Ireland which was leased by the Midland Great Western Railway (MGWR) from 1853 to 1860 in order to compete with the Great Southern & Western Railway (GSWR) whose main line through Kildare ran roughly parallel to the canal (Delany and Delany 1966, p.88). The MGWR stepped in when the Grand Canal Company was struggling to get the GSWR to take it over, but the two railway companies reached an understanding whereby the GSWR would advance to Athlone (but no further) while the MGWR would restrict its project for a branch to

Tullamore to Clara only. The canal became irrelevant and neither company pursued the matter of a takeover. When the MGWR lease expired in 1860 they both made accommodations with the canal company as compensation for the fact that it had been a pawn in their struggle (Delany 1973, pp.181–6). However, since the MGWR already owned the Royal Canal (following the takeover of 1845 which was calculated to provide land for the railway along the canal bank through Maynooth and Enfield and to save the canal company, which was hard pressed to compete with the Grand Canal) the railway age temporarily brought the two competing waterways into one fold with a desire to increase the commercial penetration of one and an obligation to keep the other open for navigation. Although the passenger service on the Royal Canal was closed freight continued to flow and the MGWR itself entered the carrying business between 1871 and 1886.

Perhaps the most complex issue involved the TMC which was taken over by the NSR in 1846. This action was actively sought in the belief that several railway projects affecting the Potteries (Macclesfield–Colwich, Stone–Norton Bridge, Harecastle–Crewe and North Rode–Burton on Trent) would ruin the canal. 'Faced with such a formidable challenge the canal company decided that instead of opposing the bill they would seek to be taken over by the railway' (Lindsay 1979, p.116). Parliament ensured that the canal would be kept 'dredged cleaned and scoured', but this was no great hardship to the NSR which was able to use the canal to transport freight to Liverpool independently of the LNWR. It placed the NSR in a stronger position during amalgamation negotiations with the LNWR such as were conducted in 1851. The failure of the ensuing parliamentary bill was due in no small measure to the opposition of canal interests that saw an LNWR monopoly arising out of any merger and wished to preserve 'a competing route to the north' (Lindsay 1979, pp.124–5). So the LNWR was thwarted; but with its interest in the Shropshire Canal, whose foothold on the Mersey at Ellesmere Port was enhanced by the completion of the Birmingham and Liverpool Junction (mentioned below), there was scope for competition on the waterways between the Mersey and Birmingham. Facilities at Ellesmere Port were greatly enlarged and the LNWR continued to be a substantial canal carrier (Pellow 1985; Wilson 1975).

However, much of the improvement came early in the Railway Age when the railway companies were not expanding their freight business aggressively and when the Railway Clearing House did not work particularly well. M.J. Freeman (1988, p.19) points out that it was between 1838 and 1848 that the twelve most important canals in the country increased their tonnage from 10.5 to 14.0 millions. There was also a transitional period which saw certain canals prosper through an attempt to go into the railway business. The unfortunate B.W. Cook may have been dismissed for disloyalty in 1894 for suggesting that the Watford–Foxton section of the enlarged GJC (formerly Grand Union) should be converted into a railway (see below), but in 1836 the Thames & Severn had put forward a bill for conversion to a railway in a bid to thwart the competition led by the Cheltenham & Great Western Union's broad gauge proposal. In 1840 there was enough alarm occasioned by plans for a railway from Dublin to Kilkenny and other towns in the south of Ireland for the Grand Canal company to contemplate a double track atmospheric railway along its bank from Portobello. This would go to an interchange point with the GSWR at Sallins and be leased to an operator who would pay rent plus a proportion of the receipts (Delany and Delany 1966, p.65). The alterations to bridges would have been a major problem and Portobello would not have been a very convenient terminus, all of which helped to undermine the plan. But the Manchester Bolton & Bury Canal Navigation did succeed in building a railway alongside its canal in 1838 while the Lancaster Canal leased the Lancaster & Preston Railway in 1842 and the Shropshire Union celebrated its birth (through amalgamations in 1846) with backing for the Wellington–Stafford railway (Turnock 1990, pp.103–4). However, in all these cases initiative soon passed to railway managements and it was through the initiatives of railway interests that various Scottish canals were filled in and used for railway construction (the Glasgow & South Western used the Glasgow Paisley & Johnstone Canal between Glasgow and Paisley; the Great North of Scotland built over the Aberdeenshire Canal between Aberdeen and Inverurie; while the Lanarkshire & Dunbartonshire used a section of Forth & Clyde Canal (Lindsay 1968; Vamplew 1972). The North British branch to Silloth, where a dock was opened in 1859, made use of the Carlisle Canal. Elsewhere canals at Kensington, Looe, Oakham, Pembrey and Torrington were superseded by railways.

Case Studies from Midland England

Recent research into canals in Leicestershire (Turnock 1997) provides an opportunity of looking into the contrasting fortunes of a group of three railway-owned canals and equally, a similar number of independent waterways (Fig 4.2). The former were not necessarily at a disadvantage, for all canals were left looking for a niche in the market where the railway interest was not unassailable; and while independent canals had the option of 'taking on' the competition, railway owned canals could always be used as pawns in the commercial struggles of main line railway companies. The first example concerns the Oakham Canal (opened in 1803) which became a Midland Railway target in connection with the Syston & Peterborough project whose planned route coincided with sections of the waterway. It seems that local opinion favoured the railway, especially after the canal had been forced to shut down during the dry summer of 1844, for the canal company was never able to arrange a really adequate water supply. But although the company itself was not prepared to organize any strong opposition to the proposed takeover, Lord Harborough of Stapleford Park near Melton Mowbray, who had invested in both the Oakham Canal and the Melton Mowbray Navigation (MMN), was implacably opposed to the railway and let it be known at a public meeting in

Oakham that he would 'spend one of his estates, at least, to oppose it and, if he did not then succeed, he would go and reside in Switzerland' (Tew 1984, p.86). This caused amusement at the time, but his earnestness was made clear when he used his power as proprietor of the canal towpath in the Stapleford area to prevent railway surveyors from carrying out their work. The result was a series of scuffles in November 1844, remembered as the 'Battle of Saxby Bridge' (Tew 1984, pp.86-94). Apart from prejudice, reasons for this aristocratic opposition may be sought in a perceived threat to the amenity of Stapleford Park and the impending demise of the canal company in which Lord Harborough had a substantial interest. But he was unable to prevent the passage of an act in 1845 empowering the railway takeover. The deal was completed in 1847 and the railway reached Oakham the following year.

Meanwhile, the Grantham Canal of 1797 enjoyed success in its early years but was subjected to competition from the Nottingham–Grantham railway which opened in 1851. The canal passed into the ownership of the Ambergate Company (subsequently the Great Northern Railway: GNR) three years later. It remained marginalized and, when ironstone quarrying began, the GNR built a branch line to Woolsthorpe in 1883 rather than retain the use of the canal which had initially transported the ore from Brewer's Grave when operations started in 1870. By this time the canal was suffering from inadequate maintenance and in 1873 wide boats could not proceed because of inadequate dredging. Silting was certainly seen as a problem when the Royal Commission on Canals and Inland Waterways was hearing evidence in 1909. The canal was dredged to Cropwell but weed was still a problem in the summer. This created a disincentive to use the canal since boats might have to load light while carriers had to be paid more if the silting was serious enough to call for unloading *en route*. Total traffic fell from 27,376 tons in 1888 to 18,802 in 1905 (Royal Commission 1910, para.195). Railway ownership was felt to be an impediment to effective competition for, although the GNR was not grossly negligent, it did not go out if its way to encourage traffic: 'they leave it to inertia to kill it' (Royal Commission 1909, min.34697) and 'do as little as they are absolutely obliged by pressure from outside' (Royal Commission 1909, min.34698). The canal was used for military purposes during the First World War. Men and stores were carried from Nottingham to Grantham when Alma Park Camp was occupied by the Machine Gun Corps. The Belvoir Castle Railway ceased carrying coal from the canal in 1916 and was closed down completely two years later. By the late 1920s traffic on the canal had almost ceased and there was a backlog of maintenance work. It was officially abandoned in 1936.

By contrast, the Ashby Canal showed a greater capacity for survival, despite purchase by the MR in 1846 for £110,000. The Leicester and Swannington Railway (LSR) was acquired at the same time and when it was modernized (with a deviation railway to bypass the Bagworth incline) and extended from Coalville to Burton on Trent it made a junction with the Ticknall Tramway on the Ashby Canal. The purchases were made 'to keep others away' (Hillier 1984) and consolidate the monopoly of the MR at the height of the Railway Mania when several competing lines were being considered. It is possible that the MR had ideas of converting the canal into a railway, or of building a line parallel to it (Holt 1992, p.8), with upgrading of the tramroad to Gresley Common. But it is doubtful if this was a high priority, given the financial difficulties of the 1850s. In any case, although the Ashby Canal Company was happy enough to sell, the Coventry and Oxford Canal Companies were strongly opposed and had clauses inserted to ensure the Ashby Canal would be kept in good order on a permanent basis, with tolls to be set no higher than those on the competing railway (and with a proportionate lowering of Ashby Canal tolls if the Oxford Canal was forced to reduce its own tolls to meet any diversion of coal traffic that might nevertheless take place) (Clinker and Hadfield 1958, p.70). The coal traffic actually increased under railway ownership, with the canal maintaining an important feeder role: 80,000 tons in 1845, 138,000 tons in 1862 and 153,000 tons in 1870. When the railway idea surfaced again it was for a quite separate project: the Ashby & Nuneaton Railway, opened with LNWR assistance in 1873 (Franks 1975).

Thereafter the traffic on the canal tended to fall, but there was still a substantial amount of coal carried. D.L. Franks (1975, p.8) mentions a new canal proposed in 1875 to run from Swannington to Ravenstone (with a branch to Ellistown) to join the Ashby Canal at Shackerstone. This was to complement another canal connecting the Ashby at Congerstone with the Coventry Canal at Polesworth (north of Atherstone) (Fig 4.2). The project was a response to congestion at Moira and the interest of Birmingham in drawing the area more effectively into the Black Country coal supply system which was heavily canal based. At a meeting of the Birmingham Chamber of Commerce in October 1875 it was stated that Birmingham would derive great benefit from such a canal since coal reserves in South Staffordshire were approaching exhaustion. However, it was inconceivable that the MR would have allowed the idea to go forward when there was ample capacity on its railway which was directly linked with Birmingham via Nuneaton. In any case the necessary capital was not forthcoming. By the end of the century, traffic on the Ashby Canal was in steep decline. Total annual traffic declined rapidly from an average of 127,600 tons over the decade beginning 1867 and 104,900 tons in the decade following to 55,100 for 1887–96 and 36,600 for 1897–1906 (Clinker and Hadfield, 1958 p.76).

The Ashby Canal was also reported to be in poor condition in 1909. In evidence to the Royal Commission on Canals and Inland Waterways Gordon Thomas referred to stoppages at Hinckley each night (from 8 p.m. to 5 a.m.) and on Sundays (Royal Commission 1909, min.38617). And as part of a polemic against railway owned canals he mentioned comments made in 1872 that, although the tolls were 'reasonable' the MR 'do very little at it' so that 'it is gradually getting worse and worse' (Royal Commission 1909, min.38620). The allegations of a reduced

Figure 4.2 : Canals of Leicestershire

Key to projects that were never undertaken: A) Original Ashby Canal route from the Trent to the Coventry Canal, last discussed in connection with the Commercial Canal in 1796; B) Proposed coal canal from Swannington and Ellistown to Garendon on the Coventry Canal (crossing the Ashby Canal at Shackerstone/Congerstone) mooted in 1875; C) Proposed extension of the Grantham Canal to Sleaford; D) Proposed extension of the Oakham Canal to Stamford (with an alternative link from the Old Union at Market Harborough); E) Proposed branch from Smeeton Westerby to Uppingham; F) Proposed links from the Old Union at Blaby to the Oxford Canal at Cosford near Rugby: an alternative to the Grand Union project offering links with the West Midlands as well as London; G) Original 'Old Union' line from Foxton to Northampton. H) Telford's line for a connection with the Grand Junction at Long Buckby; also including a branch from Arklingworth to Rushton near Kettering.

sectional area were refuted by the MR (Royal Commission 1910, para.140), but Thomas was not alone in expressing dissatisfaction because R.D. Waddell of Measham Collieries thought the canal was in a poor condition due to silting. When his company had introduced its own boats it found the canal was dirty, but no satisfaction was gained from the canal company (Royal Commission 1909, min.39048). Dredging was inadequate and because of mud and weeds it was difficult for boats to pass. One five mile section was particularly difficult, with boats touching the bottom at all times and boatmen always needed a great deal of local knowledge to appreciate the effective depth. The Royal Commission evidently accepted the evidence about poor maintenance. They concluded that the Ashby Canal 'should be a very big feeder of traffic to the Grand Junction system, but by reason of reduced sectional area and the difficulty boats have in navigating the canal there is a very small traffic indeed coming from the collieries situated on that canal' (Royal Commission 1907, min.19282).

The parliamentary act requiring adequate maintenance was not being complied with, for although the canal should have been accessible to boats carrying 40 tons, 30 tons was the norm and even by this standard loading might have to be up to five or six tons light, especially during the summer months. So, against the 40 ton standard the actual loadings might be as much as 40 percent down; yet the boatmen expected the same payment (Royal Commission 1909, min.39079). The Measham company came to the conclusion that the canal was in 'such a bad state' it would take years to improve the navigation, so a rail connection was installed (Royal Commission 1909, min.39045). The railway siding was duly completed in 1902 (Royal Commission 1910, para.140). However the Measham Colliery Company still saw an improved canal to London as a great potential benefit to their coal trade.

There was likewise a sense of opportunity for the brick and terracotta trade which had also abandoned the canal, though activity was further constrained by competition from new works at Peterborough, set up 'on account of the high cost of getting the bricks away from the Measham district [which] has practically stopped the industry' (Royal Commission 1909, min.39149). The industry could revive because the area possesses the 'finest deposit of clay in Great Britain for that particular class of goods and plenty of it' (Royal Commission 1909, min.39151).

Independent canals: Melton Mowbray Navigation and the Nutbrook Canal

The independent Melton Mowbray Navigation of 1797 was heavily affected by the railway between Syston and Peterborough although a bend near Thrussington had to be straightened and a large loop was cut off at Brooksby, shortening the navigation by about a tenth of a mile, (Miller and Fletcher 1984). But there was a sharp reduction in freight from 68,900 tons in 1847 to 13,300 in 1850 and 11,000 in

1868. The company made drastic toll reductions (from 2s.6d. to just 6d. per ton) and cutbacks in maintenance in order to retain some traffic. But the situation could not be sustained and, after unsuccessfully seeking a takeover by first the Loughborough Navigation and then the MR, the company was forced to apply for an act of abandonment in 1877. Yet it was a significant achievement for the MMN to have carried on as an independent company for some thirty years after the opening of the railway.

Built as an independent branch of the Erewash Canal during the years 1793–96 (Stevenson 1970) (Fig 4.3), the Nutbrook Canal provides a good example of the complexities of the Railway Age. It was only four and a half miles long but had 13 locks supplied with water by the 'old' reservoir suite at Shipley (immediately above the canal terminus) and a 'new' reservoir at Mapperley built in one of the tributary valleys in 1821 (Stevenson 1970, pp. 40–7). The canal was intended to be an adjunct to the West Hallam & Shipley Collieries, carrying coal, iron and limestone, and had been advocated strongly by the Mundy family of Shipley Hall, but its properties passed to Shipley Collieries and later to Stanton Ironworks. Inspired by the demand for coal in Nottingham which had first given rise to the Ilkeston and Nottingham turnpike (1764) and the Erewash Canal, which was open to Langley Mill in 1779, the Nutbrook Canal served a small mining district with several wagonways to connect the collieries with the canal (although Shipley Collieries also gave themselves the option of using the Erewash Canal through the wagonway to Shipley Gate). As the canal network was enlarged the markets for the coal began to take in a variety of destinations along the Grand Union and Grand Junction canals with the stimulus of some toll reductions (drawbacks) to stimulate trade with other waterways. Limestone was burnt in kilns at Shipley and West Hallam and a supply of both coal and limestone was maintained to the Stanton Ironworks when it opened in 1798. The idea was to exploit the ironstone found on the Stanhope estate and to generate more traffic for the canal. Traffic on the canal grew from an annual average of 44,700 tons between 1794 and 1809 to 45,300 and 64,500 during the 1810s and 1820s respectively. Revenue increased from £1,430 to £1,500 and £2,060 (Stevenson 1970, pp.142–7).

The situation was transformed first by the LSR and the Midland Counties Railway (MCR). The former generated stiff competition for Erewash coal in general while the latter, although calculated to cope with the threat to local coal interests, threatened the canal's position. Opposition to railways prevented construction along the Erewash valley for a few years, but the Nutbrook company was forced to reduce its tolls and 'after August 1832 no coals ever again paid the maximum tonnage of 8d.' (Stevenson 1970, p.75). However the Erewash Valley railway was built in 1847, and although its route avoided difficulty at the junction of the Erewash and Nutbrook canals, there was immediate construction of a branch (Mundy's Railway) from Shipley Gate to the collieries situated at the head of the canal. Both the main line and branch were being built in 1847. The branch followed close to the line of a

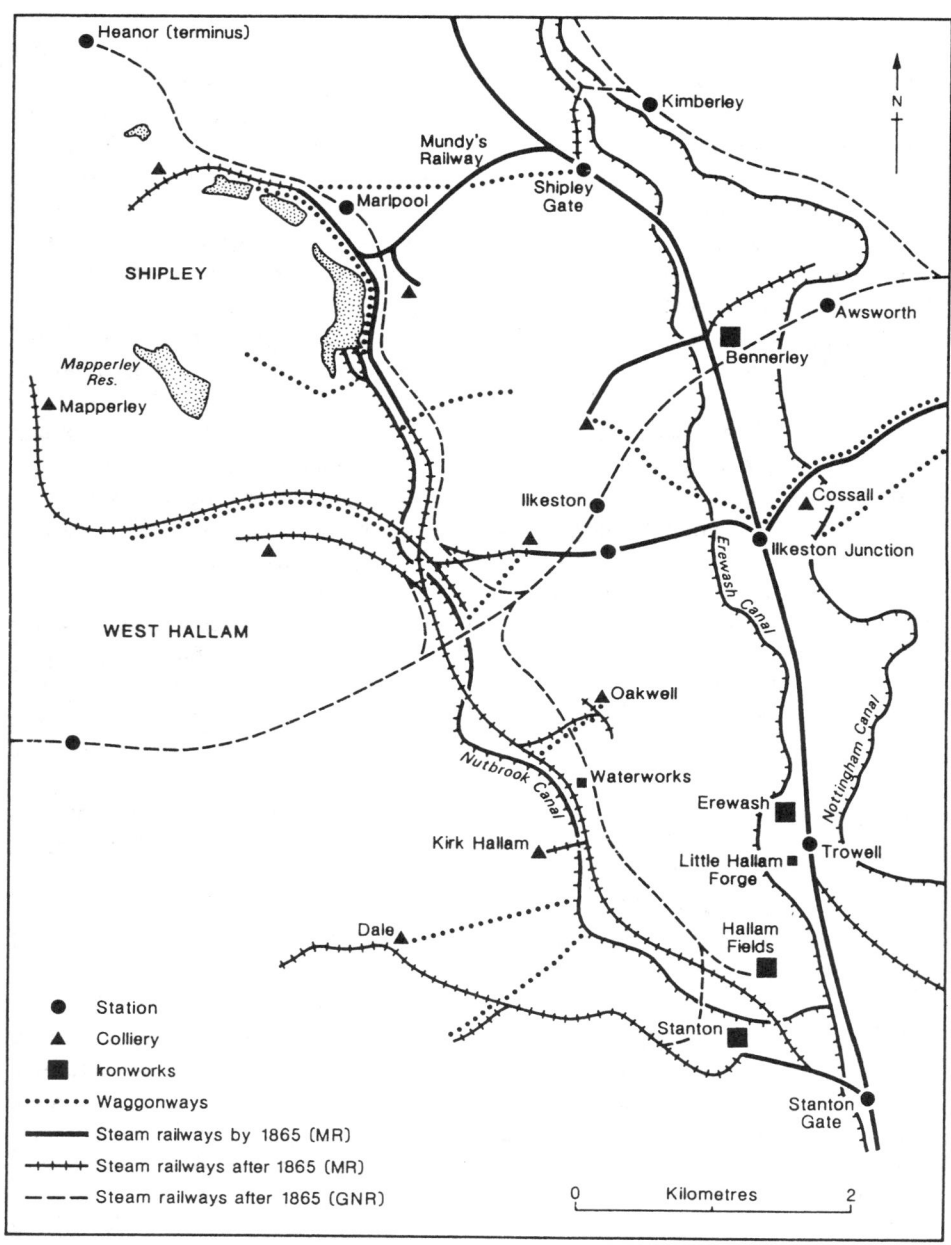

Figure 4.3: The Nutbrook Canal

wagonway and was steeply graded, but it provided an alternative means of export and part of the cost was met by the Mundy family (especially with regard to a new incline to cross the old wooden line to the Erewash Canal), although they had interests in the Nutbrook Canal as well. The railway enabled pressure to be exerted to secure a reduction in tolls for Shipley coal and a general willingness to be more competitive helped to attract a new ironworks to West Hallam, with favourable rates for both the raw materials and the outward movement of iron products. This venture of 1845 represented the reappearance of an iron industry on the Stanhope estate following the shortlived venture of 1798–1805 (Stevenson 1970, pp.70–9). Since the local industries generally operated their own fleets on the canal there was always a good reason to stay with the canal if adequate concessions could be obtained. In 1821 for example the Mundys had over 20 narrow boats working through to the GJC from Shipley Wharf and there were still at least 15 in 1835.

The canal proprietors seemed keener to give way to the railway, at least initially. Although traffic increased by 53.1 per cent between the 1830s and 1850s, revenue fell by 11.4 per cent (Stevenson 1970, pp.142–7). In 1845 they contemplated a Nutbrook Valley Mineral Railway that would replace the canal in its entirety. It was not proposed that the line would be built on the bed of the canal or that the canal company would be formally involved, but some owners were of the opinion that they should sell out to any company that might propose to duplicate the service provided by the canal. However no further action was taken and some districts served by the canal, such as West Hallam, had no railway service until the MR's Nutbrook and Shipley branch was completed from Stanton Gate in 1870 (Stevenson 1970, pp.76–81). This involved the extension of a short branch which served the Stanton Ironworks in 1847 (contemporaneously with the construction of the main line along the Erewash Valley). This did not mean there was any immediate abandonment of the canal and as the local ironstone was exhausted, material was brought in by canal from Blisworth from 1853, where the company carried out its own quarry operations, with canal transport to the furnaces. But since the expansion of the plant meant that the old side basin had to be filled in, boats were unloaded in the main channel and after 1870 larger amounts of ironstone were brought in from the Wellingborough area (including Desborough and Finedon). This involved using the MR since there was no convenient canal link available. By this time the canal company was embarrassed by the very slender profit margins as more and more of the receipts were taken up by expenses, and 'the company's real trouble began when mining encroached beneath its canal works' leading to serious problems of seepage from the old reservoir at Shipley (Stevenson 1970, p.82). Both traffic and revenue were now falling quite sharply (Stevenson 1970, pp.142–7).

Any commitment to heavy expenditure was discouraged by the railway extension from Stanton Gate and the branches which were built simultaneously to the Manners, Mapperley and West Hallam collieries as well as to Kirk Hallam in 1878. Further embarrassment arose in the same year through the construction of the

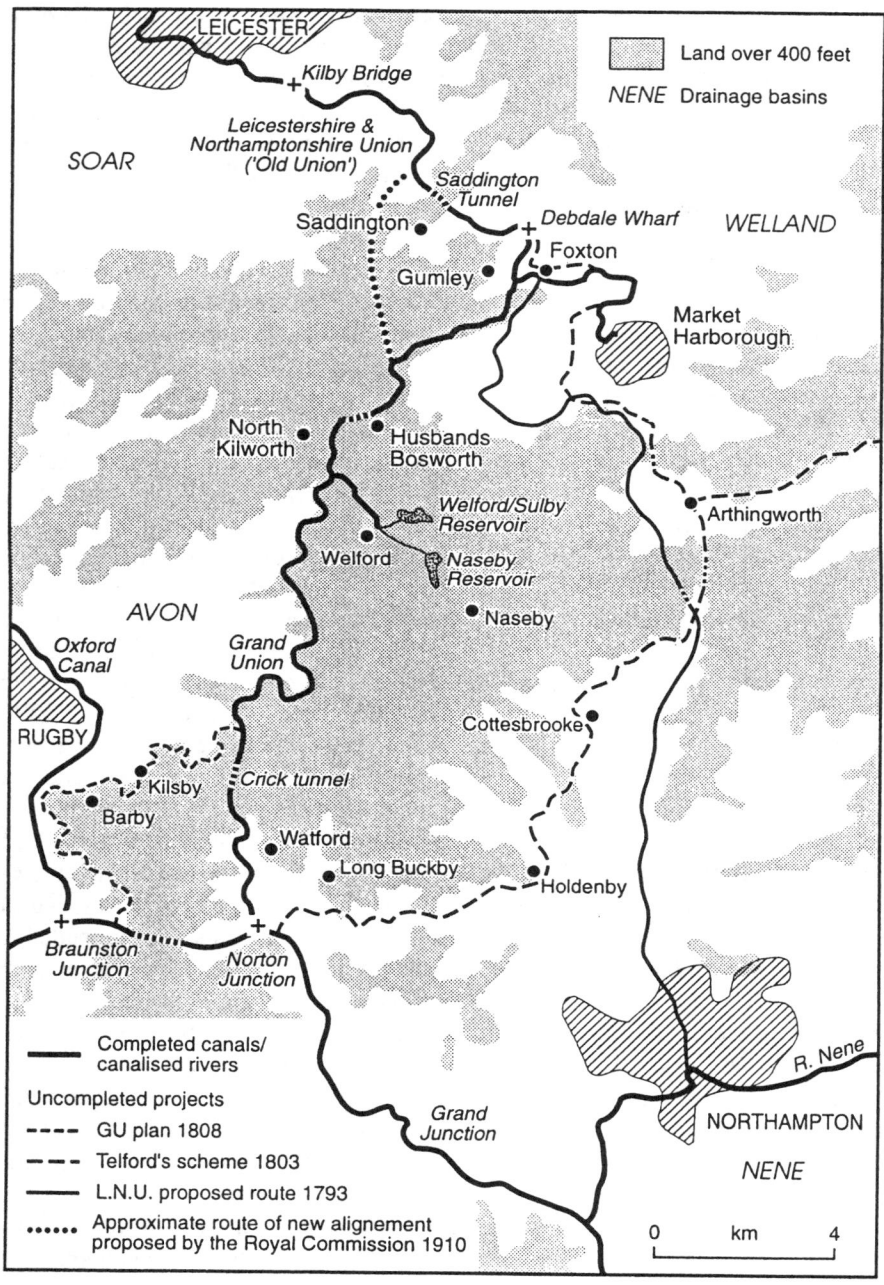

Figure 4.4: Union canals and their connection with the Grand Junction Canal's Braunston Summit

GNR's Derbyshire & Staffordshire Extension which crossed the canal at Moor's Bridge and threw off branches to Nutbrook and West Hallam pits. This was also the time when the Stanton Ironworks ceased making regular use of the canal. The Nutbrook Canal now seriously sought a railway company takeover but there was no interest; and the GNR Heanor branch, projected in 1882, adopted a route parallel to the canal past the Shipley reservoir. Serious water supply problems arose during the 1880s and maintenance work proved inadequate. The last dividend was paid in 1885 and by the end of the decade costs exceeded income. Application for formal closure was considered in 1900, but rejected. The canal was reported derelict in 1907 apart from some traffic from Stanton (Stevenson 1970, p.119). Its demise highlights again how the reduction in income with the onset of railway competition was related in the long term to maintenance problems and an inability to contemplate any substantial development. Reductions in dividends eroded confidence among shareholders and increased the attractiveness of absorption into a more profitable railway business which in this case was not achieved.

Independent Canals: Grand Junction Canal

The final example takes the 'main line' comprising the GJC and the Union Canals: both the Old Union (OUC) from Leicester to Market Harborough and the GUC from Foxton to Norton Junction (Fig 4.4). Cumulatively, these canals provided a link between London and Leicester which was completed in 1815. Here, the effect of railway development was felt almost immediately with the opening of early inter-city railways like the LBR and the MCR. However, the LSR, a local mineral line, did have some positive impact despite its devastating effect on the profits of the Leicester and Loughborough Navigations since coal was transferred to the canal at Leicester West Bridge. Chandler (1958, p.30) reports that 80,000 tons of coal were transferred to the Union Canals in 1845. To hold on to this through traffic the GUC reduced its tolls on traffic heading for the GJC in the 1850s. The carrying trade continued with difficulty, for there was a decline in all traffic and not just in coal. In 1840 James Sutton and Company gave up their boats in favour of forwarding from Leicester to the north by rail (Stevens 1992, p.69). And Pickfords ceased using the GJC and the GUC in 1847. There was some modernization, for firms like Walker and Stubbs in Market Harborough were advertising fly boats to all parts of the country and steam powered vessels were coming into use around mid century, although speed limits were strictly enforced in order to prevent serious damage to the banks. But the trend was inexorably downwards. Loughborough Navigation shares, once worth £4,000, stood at only £100 at the turn of the century because 'a great fall took place when the MR was opened' and the price 'has dropped gradually since' (Royal Commission 1909, mins.38418–23).

The entire line of canals from the Erewash to the GJC was strong enough to remain independent of the railways, although government did not choose to facilitate amalgamation. However, in 1894 some rationalization did take place with an amalgamation of the GJC, GUC and OUC companies 'as a preliminary to a last great effort to compete in the Nottinghamshire and Derbyshire coal trade' (Hadfield 1966, p.186): the inclined plane opened at Foxton in 1900. For the general gloom of the stagnation of the late nineteenth century was belatedly overtaken by a mood of optimism due initially to the psychological boost that came from the Manchester Ship Canal, opened in 1894. Although this canal had little to do with inland navigation, it demonstrated that waterways still had a place in investment programmes. The late 1890s was a period of economic boom, especially during the years 1897–1900, and the annual growth in gross national product by 2.1 per cent was the best performance over the half century prior to the First World War. As industrial production increased there was a growth in traffic for the canals as well as the railways. The increase in waterway traffic was very slight overall (33.1 million tons in 1888 rising to 34.0 in 1898 before falling back to 32.3 in 1905); but the GJC did particularly well with an increase from 1.17 to 1.62 million tons from 1888 to 1898, with a further rise to 1.79 million tons in 1905. This was reflected in toll revenue and generated optimism. Hence the belief that if only capacity could be increased it would be possible to make toll reductions and compete effectively with the railway. Lower canal tolls might well divert a significant amount of coal traffic moving south and merchandise from London docks in the opposite direction. Of course there were assumptions that the railways would 'allow' this to happen, an attitude which showed over reliance on government willingness to insist on free competition, and that the economy would continue to experience boom conditions.

Creation of the enlarged company led to renewed interest in the coal trade from the Erewash Valley. Indeed the amalgamations were ultimately extended to the Erewash Canal and Loughborough–Leicester Navigations in 1932. Of course the company had no means of knowing that the internal combustion engine would soon revolutionize freight transport for the second time; and so they had every reason to suppose that canals would continue to have a significant commercial role. Yet even so, the railways would surely remain in a very strong position especially with an enhanced capacity for moving coal from the East Midlands to London as a result of the opening of the GCR in 1899, duplicating the services already provided by the MR. But confidence was sustained by the fact that railway company dividends had lost some of their buoyancy as a result of heavy investment in new lines and equipment, while railway rates were widely considered to be excessively high and a heavy burden on industrial areas like Birmingham. The GJC engineer Gordon Thomas was allowed to go ahead and install an inclined plane at Foxton which avoided the delays frequently encountered at Foxton Locks and also opened the way for wide boats to use the Foxton summit provided Watford Locks were widened as well.

Water supply was an important consideration, because Foxton water at 412 feet could feed into the slightly lower Braunston summit at just over 358.2 feet which was a critical section on the GJC route to Birmingham, due to its short length and limited reservoir capacity. It was always the case that water from the Foxton summit cascading through Watford locks helped to maintain the level at Norton Junction. But there was always the possibility that the reservoirs on the Foxton summit could be used entirely for the benefit of the Braunston summit if losses at the Foxton end were eliminated. This was no doubt one reason why B.W. Cook, the company's engineer at Blisworth, suggested in 1894 that the entire 'Leicester Line' might be converted into a railway (Goodwin 1987). According to this plan there would be inclines on either side of the Foxton summit, though with gradients of around 1 in 100 these would, presumably, have been negotiable by locomotives and others on the descent to Leicester. Boats would be carried on bogie trucks made up into trainloads of up to 400 tons hauled by freight locomotives similar to a type used on the LNWR, with which there would be a physical connection at Watford, complementing the proposed link with the MR in Leicester (Goodwin 1988, p.21). The company was not amused and it was sad that Cook felt obliged to leave its employment for his indiscretion in casting doubt on the efficiency of conventional waterways, for he was reacting to the very real problem of summit level water supply as a constraint on the growth of traffic. It was left to his successors, notably T.W. Millner, to find other solutions.

A number of improvements followed, including back pumping at each lock on the descent from the Braunston summit through Long Buckby. But more water could also be obtained by back pumping from the bottom of the locks in Braunston and here the old pumping equipment, which had been installed in 1810 in the shape of a Boulton & Watt steam engine, following initial use of a portable engine from Blisworth Tunnel, was replaced in 1897 by a new Gwynnes steam engine, capable of pumping three to four lock fulls of water per hour. This equipment pumped water discharged from the bottom lock into low level reservoirs beside the pumphouse. Additional water had to be purchased from the Oxford Canal as part of the back pumping operation. Meanwhile, the depth of water along the summit section was increased by one foot in order to hold more water: one inch of summit water would fill 10 locks (Goodwin 1988, p.50). It is understandable that fuller use of the Foxton level reservoirs at Braunston was seen as an attractive prospect and one that could more easily be realized as a result of the 1894 amalgamation which occurred, significantly, during the period of intensive pumping activity at Braunston.

Of course, in terms of water supply it would have been much cheaper for back pumping to have taken place at Foxton, for one inclined plane in isolation could never have been profitable. Instead, the investment at Foxton must be seen as part of a wider plan for modernization of the entire route to London. If such a plan was to be undertaken, Foxton was probably the best place to start and it was presumably born out of the growth scenario of the 1890s, which was subsequently outlined in evidence to the Royal Commission. Boats with capacity up to 100 tons might be used and the canal would be 45 feet wide to allow wide boats, or pairs of narrow boats side by side, to pass each other. The Commission adopted the Thomas-inclined plane model and sought to apply it to a network of canals connecting the Midlands not only with London but also the Humber, Mersey and Severn estuary. They probably exaggerated the benefits of canal refurbishment but nevertheless 'there is a strong probability that canals freed from railway company ownership would have been cheaper and more efficient competitors for bulk freight' (Cain 1988, p.94). However, the government refused to back the Commission's call for investment and it is significant that as soon as this decision was made the Foxton inclined plane was closed.

Conclusion

This paper has attempted a baseline review of the impact of the Railway Age on the British canal system. The picture that emerges is one of local variation despite the underlying trends which affected the whole country by virtue of the technology available and the legislative framework which regulated the interactions between rail and canal interests. Clearly, there is more to be done in reconstructing the business environment in general and the responses by influential individuals who seem to have been pessimistic over the prospects for canals. The steam railway era saw investment in new canals forced to a standstill by the middle of the nineteenth century. Some canals were totally eliminated by railway competition, while others were, more or less, happy to be taken over by railway companies, mainly during the 1840s, 1850s and 1860s. Canals in the north west seem to have been particularly prone to railway takeover. However, a considerable number continued to operate as independent companies and were still carrying substantial amounts of traffic at the end of the century. Railway ownership imposed constraints in the sense that no initiatives could be taken which could damage the owner's railway business, although this is not to say that canals were denied a useful role. The situation relating to the Ashby Canal was repeated on many other railway owned canals, especially in Birmingham, and it could be argued that legal requirements to maintain waterways in good working order encouraged railway owners to make a virtue out of necessity. Independent canals were by no means guaranteed a future as the MMN and Nutbrook cases make clear. Other branch canals suffered the same fate, though not always as a result of railway competition: the Leicester Navigation's 'Forest Line' was a casualty of difficult trading conditions at the onset of the Napoleonic wars. But there was at least the possibility of competition with railways as the case of GJC makes clear.

Although some improvement may have been possible as a basis for survival, there seemed no possibility of any significant expansion of the canal network. The

Birmingham & Liverpool Junction Canal was authorized in 1826 and opened in 1835, just in time to avoid the depression in canal building as capital was diverted to the more profitable railways in the wake of the Liverpool & Manchester and London & Birmingham successes. Further provision of cross country links was ruled out and the Midland canals remained isolated from both East Anglia and South Wales. In the case of East Anglia, the navigable Nene is accessible through the Northampton branch of the GJC (today's 'Grand Union') and there are links across the Fens to the Ouse at Denver, but no connection exists further east to the Waveney and Yare valleys. Plans to extend from either Oakham or Smeeton Westerby to the Welland at Stamford and to connect the Ouse with the Waveney were never carried out. Nor were those for the Kington & Leominster Canal in the Welsh Marches which would have connected the Severn near Stourport with South Wales using the tramroad from Kington to Hay and Brecon to connect with the Brecknock & Abergavenny and Monmouthshire canals. Not even the existing waterway system could remain commercially effective throughout. Parliamentary goodwill was forthcoming through encouragement to amalgamate, reduce tolls and borrow money for modernization as well as for canal companies to become carriers on their own waterways, reversing the prohibition in force until 1845. But this could not overcome the serious inadequacies of certain parts of the system.

At the end of the century there was a sense of a new opportunity as mechanical power was harnessed to canal transport. Railway profits were depressed in the 1890s due to heavy investment, while a boom in trade gave the canal companies a growing income just at the time when the Manchester Ship Canal (1894) showed what new technology could achieve. A Royal Commission looked closely at the canals and underlined the general problem arising through the lack of a common gauge and the cost of increasing capacity across the 'grand ridge': a broad reference to the scarplands that canals between the Midlands and London had to negotiate, and which seriously complicated most canal movements between the main river basins. In the context of the 'grand cross' – the basis of the national canal network linking the Humber, Mersey, Severn and Thames through the Coventry, Oxford, Staffordshire & Worcestershire and Trent & Mersey canals – the scarplands of the south Midlands were particularly challenging in terms of water supply. The Royal Commission backed the improvements which had been started on the GJC and envisaged government help for a revamping of the system. For although the canal companies were generally too weak to inspire confidence among the investing public, state support to increase capacity in terms of individual boatloads and annual traffic and to speed up journeys could have been the key to increased canal usage that would have provided more toll revenue to finance further improvements. This would have allowed some reduction in toll levels as an incentive to a further diversion of freight from the railways to the canals, but government help was refused and by the First World War it was clear that resuscitation of canals in general and improved capacity over the 'grand ridge' in particular was economically unviable. The railway's advantage over the canals was confirmed.

Chapter Five

Railway Architecture, Architects and Engineers.

Gordon Biddle

There is a curious void in railway histories. They go into great detail about promotion, formation, construction and operation of railways, and even more about locomotives and rolling stock, almost down to the last rivet. The same is true about specialist books on locomotives and train working. The void largely comprises the subjects in this book. True, they have received a certain amount of treatment in recent years, principally by the authors, but by comparison there is still a very marked shortfall in knowledge of what the railways did, how they performed as businesses, and the effect they had on landscapes, towns and cities, and people. Jack Simmons has provided invaluable service in three books (Simmons 1978, 1986, 1991) that treat these and other aspects as a coherent whole, but he generally finishes around 1914, and on such a vast canvas has been able to do little more than give examples which, it is hoped, other historians will pursue in greater depth.

Here the subject is the buildings and structures that made up the most visible part of the railway; the first identifiable objects that the traveller sees, whether going for a train or passing by on a road. Perhaps, because they are so obvious, they are taken for granted, with little questioning of why they are in a particular place and form. Yet, despite now being virtually the only physical remains we have of the railway as it was in its heyday, outside museums and the privately preserved lines, we know less about them than many other features that are long gone; although in the past few years there has been a welcome increase in published material. There is still much to find, the extent of which can be put in a series of questions with, in some cases, the answers. Those which so far have none will, perhaps, stimulate research; for, as will be shown, what we can learn about the structural environment of the railway has a direct relationship to how we treat it.

The main questions are interrelated: *what*? *why*? and *who*? The first is the easiest. What is meant here by railway architecture is structures of all kinds: bridges; viaducts; tunnels; stations in all their enormous multiplicity of shapes and sizes; hotels; goods sheds and warehouses (a much neglected subject); engine sheds (now becoming extinct); signal boxes (likewise); houses, of which the railways had some 58,000 occupied by employees alone; and a host of miscellaneous buildings. Space precludes more than considering the first four, but they will serve as examples.

That is the easy question. Next, *why* were they built as they are? Again taking the easiest first, the grandeur of arched viaducts in brick or stone spoke eloquently without embellishment, with certain exceptions for some of which we know the reasons. Robert Stephenson's tubular bridge at Conway, for instance, was given castellated portals by the architect Francis Thompson in order to comply with the Chester & Holyhead Railway's Act which required it to sit as harmoniously as possible beside the castle. But there were no such requirements for the much larger Britannia tubular bridge over the Menai Strait; yet the railway went to the expense of commissioning Thompson to design the piers in Egyptian style with Grecian detailing, and John Thomas the sculptor to carve the stone lions guarding the approaches. Why? In the absence of any other reason the answer can only be what has been stated elsewhere: pride – justifiably so for such a pioneering bridge – and expression, just like the London & Birmingham with its giant portico at Euston.

The gothic crenellations applied to the viaduct in the Pass of Killiecrankie on the Highland Railway in Perthshire, and the latticed girder bridge over the River Tilt at Blair Atholl – among others in Scotland – were designed to give substance to the placatory words of the engineer Joseph Mitchell when he persuaded the Duke of Atholl to accept the railway; a concession frequently made to powerful landlords. But why was this seeming extravagance applied to Gauxholme Viaduct, an iron and stone structure in the narrow valley of the Calder in West Yorkshire? It was, and is, a dramatic location, despite industrialization, but was that sufficient to sway the Manchester & Leeds Railway, a company not exactly flush with cash in 1840? Even more extravagant were the classical balustrades and end pavilions specially commissioned for the Ouse Valley Viaduct in Sussex by the London & Brighton Railway from David Mocatta, who designed its stations. Yet the other viaducts on this line are relatively plain. The turrets adorning Knucklas Viaduct on the Central Wales Railway where it borders remotest Radnorshire are also splendid; or the battlements on the Lledr Viaduct on the Conway Valley line; and other later examples elsewhere, after the first flushes of achievement had faded.

Embellishments on brick or stone bridges are less common; perhaps because there are so many more of them. What there are, generally, were done at the request of a landowner, and the most elaborate is probably the underbridge in Shugborough Park, Staffordshire, which was decorated with balustrades, heraldic devices and other insignia of the Earl of Lichfield. Not far away, a bridge over the North Staffordshire Railway at Sandon bears the arms of the Earls Harrowby, several of whom were on the company's board. The bridge was raised for electrification work in the 1960s, but someone was thoughtful enough to retain the coat of arms. The nearby station itself, also specially designed, reflected the style of the gate lodges at Sandon Hall, just up the road.

On the Coventry to Leamington line there are two examples only a few miles apart. An underbridge bears the arms of the Gregorys of Stivichall Manor where they are easily seen from below, but the other one is less easily explained because it is just an accommodation bridge over the railway, on which the arms of the Leighs of Stoneleigh Abbey can only be seen by careful observation from a passing train. Arms that the author has not identified adorn the short viaduct at the foot of the Falls of Cruachan alongside Loch Awe, on the Callander & Oban Railway, and no doubt there are numbers of others.

Many iron plate girder bridges bear decorative designs cast into the parapets. Some have the classical simplicity of squares and rectangles, perhaps with rounded or concave corners, while others are more complex. One of the most intricate carries Middlesbrough station over a street and also bears the North Eastern Railway's initials, the date and its name: Albert Bridge. Today the value of these bridges in the urban scene is acknowledged by picking out the design in contrasting colours, some tasteful, others less so, but all of them enlivening the townscape and certainly an improvement on the old battleship grey or oxide red. Variegated painting is not new, of course; paint scrapes can reveal earlier colour schemes, prompting commendable efforts to reproduce them, as the preserved Severn Valley Railway has done on the very fine iron-arched Victoria Bridge over the River Severn at Arley. In erecting these elaborate bridges compared with plain plate the railways incurred considerable extra expense on the drawing board, in the pattern making shop and in the foundry, (even though the design may have come from an ironfounder's pattern book), stemming from motives of pride, whether in achievement, a national event, or of self-advertisement of the railway, the foundry or both. In instances like these, secreted in minute books or local newspaper files there may be found other real reasons.

Tunnel portals were enhanced for similarly different motives. The massive wing walls, buttresses and classical overtones of the south end of Primrose Hill Tunnel, a mile from Euston, were the direct result of a clause in the London & Birmingham Railway's Act obtained by Eton College, which owned the land above, as a safeguard against collapse so that house building could begin. Without it, an open cutting could have been made. Significantly, the northern portal, hidden in a cutting, is quite plain. The same railway provides other examples of tunnels with dissimilar portals. The pediment on the original Watford Tunnel was to help appease the Earl of Essex at whose insistence the tunnel was built, but at others the reason is less clear. Both ends of Northchurch and Stowe Hill are relatively plain. The London end of Lislade is in stone with heavy rustication, but the portal at the other end, which can be seen from an adjacent bridge, is on red brick, elaborate turrets and crenellations in blue that appear to date from the second of the two newer tunnels, built for the widening of 1876. They may, of course, have replaced similar earlier work. The other tunnels, although monumental in stone, are plainer. The north end of Kilsby, again close to a main road, has a heavily dentilled cornice, and the tops of the two prominent main working shafts are crenellated, doubtless to improve their appearance. Both ends of Beechwood, also close to road bridges, are similar to each other.

The decorative portals of Shugborough Tunnel are easier to explain. Egyptian at one end and Norman at the other, they were designed, like the bridge, expressly for the Earl of Lichfield. So were the excessively ornate tunnel mouths at Audley End and Littlebury on the Eastern Counties Railway (ECR), to accommodate Lord Braybrooke, one including his coat of arms on the keystone – but only at the south ends. All these examples are away from public view. Likewise at Bramhope, on the Leeds and Thirsk Railway, the highly decorated north portal was probably provided to placate the landowner (Sheeran 1994, pp.111–12).

At Box Tunnel, on the Great Western, Brunel gave fine classical dignity to the western portal, close to the Bath road, but the eastern end, buried in a cutting, was left plain. Yet his tunnels between Bath and Bristol had decorative entrances, except the east end of Bristol Number Three which was bare rock, although only the eastern end of Twerton Tunnel could be seen from the road.

Again, the turrets and castellations on the north end of Clayton Tunnel in Sussex, and Red Hill Tunnel overlooking the Trent and the complimentary Gothic styled bridge, on the Nottinghamshire–Derbyshire border, were prominent features justifying the effort. So one can perhaps conclude that where there was no landowning or other important interest to satisfy, tunnel entrances that could be seen from a road or were prominent in the landscape were embellished for effect, which leaves the question why so much was expended on hidden tunnels like Brunel's between Bristol and Bath and, more intriguingly, one end only at Sough near Darwen, which is in a deep cutting far from a road - the pride of the engineer who wished to express it in his work, but could only carry his board of directors so far?

Certainly there was desire to impart an appearance of strength and solidity in works of this kind, partly in order to reassure timid passengers unaccustomed to the new form of travel, and Gothic was a style well suited to convey it. Further, it was currently fashionable in artistic circles, and so far as third class passengers were concerned tunnel portals could easily be seen from the open carriages, although not from the enclosed first and second class, which had quite small windows. By and large historians have not sought answers to these questions, yet the works are large, noble and likely to interest the man in the street. We do not make enough of them.

The third and largest question, *who?*, refers to the designer, and here we are principally concerned with stations. The architects of many are known, and the best known names are well documented: the Hardwicks, Brunel, Tite, the Barrys, Scott. But there are numbers where the degree of collaboration between engineers, architects, consultants and contractors is uncertain or subject to argument, and even more where the designer is as yet unknown.

Railway building produced interesting associations of disciplines, some long standing. One of the most enduring was between the engineer Joseph Locke, the architect William Tite, and the contractors William Mackenzie and Thomas Brassey. They had partners from time to time: J.E. Errington with Locke, Edward N. Clifton with Tite, and John Stephenson with Mackenzie and Brassey. The names of the three, or four, principals occur together repeatedly: on the London & Southampton and its successor the London & South Western, the Lancaster & Carlisle, the Caledonian, the Scottish Central, and the Scottish Midland Junction Railways; and on the Paris–Rouen and Paris–Havre lines in France.

Tite is a particularly fascinating character. After an initial flirtation with the Great Western, for which he bought its first office in London and was one of the directors named in its Act, he acted as architect, surveyor and land agent for the London & South Western (LSWR) for upwards of thirty-three years. He designed the original termini, several other important stations, and an evolving dynasty of wayside stations as the railway fought its way westwards. There is, for instance, a strong similarity between his Lancaster & Carlisle and Caledonian stations and those on the Southampton & Dorchester and North Devon Railways; and between Carlisle and Perth. His surviving stations in northern France can also be identified with styles he adopted in Britain.

A man of great versatility and energy, Tite died childless and, unfortunately, so far as is known he left no family papers. His best biography is therefore brief (Briggs 1950). At the head of his profession for many years, he became well established before the age of thirty and built up one of the first of the large Victorian practices. He is best known for rebuilding the Royal Exchange in the City of London in 1844, and he also designed churches, public buildings and houses. He was a prominent valuer and was much sought after as an arbitrator, particularly by railways. In addition to the LSWR, he acted for the London & Blackwall, ECR, Great Eastern, and London Tilbury & Southend (LTSR) companies, was also a director of the ECR, and was chairman of the North Devon. He invested widely in railways and was not above turning his positions to his own advantage. He was involved in the dubious practices of the contractors Peto Brassey & Betts during their lease of the LTSR; his part in the famous compensation dispute between the ECR and Lord Petre is far from clear; and the way in which he gained the Royal Exchange commission was questioned at the time.

For all that, he gained a knighthood, was a director of two banks, twice president of the Royal Institute of British Architects (uniquely), a Fellow of the Royal Society, and MP for Bath for seventeen years, although curiously there appear to be no papers about his activities in the city's records (Information from D. Brooke). He never shrank from speaking in the House on any subject on which he had views, which were many; he served on select committees; and he played a leading part in the controversy between Gilbert Scott (who wrote approvingly of his stations) and Palmerston over the designs for the Foreign Office in Whitehall: on the side of Palmerston. His passions were archaeology and collecting fine art, and at his death in 1873 at the age of 75 he left £400,000: by today's figures, more than a few millions. Strong meat for a biographer.

Tite has been mentioned more extensively as an example of what can lie behind a railway architect. The recent deposit in the Institution of Civil Engineers' library of a very large collection of hitherto unknown diaries, notebooks and papers of William Mackenzie will undoubtedly throw new light on many of his contemporaries, including Tite. We have already had a taste (Murphy 1994); more is eagerly awaited. For someone of his forceful character it seems he is likely to emerge more a partner of Locke, Brassey and Mackenzie than in the somewhat subservient role it has been inferred he occupied in 1846 at a time of his rapidly growing influence, two years after he had finished the Royal Exchange (Haworth 1994, p.69 n.246).

Relationships between other engineers and architects are equally worthy of study, not least the question of who was the architect's principal: railway company, engineer or, occasionally, contractor. It is often far from clear. Brunel was his own architect for much of his early work, and no mean one at that; but for the decorative treatment of the Paddington trainshed he did not hesitate to call on Matthew Digby Wyatt, for whom he had great respect, and Wyatt's work made all the difference. It also seems that Francis Thompson may have designed the houses in the new town at Swindon, so often attributed to Brunel, and the elaborate station refreshment interior depicted in a contemporary print (Bristol University library, Brunel's private letter book, 26, 10 January 1842, fol. 249).

T.M. Penson worked closely with Henry Robertson, engineer of the Shrewsbury & Chester and Shrewsbury & Hereford Railways. Penson, one of a family of architects from the area, who also built the picturesque stations on the Newtown & Machynlleth Railway (later Cambrian), had a lifetime of notable work that included the reintroduction of the half timbering so familiar to visitors to Chester. Robertson wrote him a warm and handsome reference which secured him the job of county surveyor for Cheshire (Biddle 1993, pp.61–71).

Fig 5.1 Medieval adornments and arms on Falls of Cruachan viaduct in 1989 (Author)

Fig 5.2 Accomodation bridge bearing the arms of the Leigh family of Stoneleigh Abbey near Kenilworth, Warwickshire, in 1953 (R.E.G.Read/Author)

Fig 5.3 The north end of Bramhope Tunnel in 1956 (Author)

Fig 5.4 The Dublin Heuston (formerly Kingsbridge) Terminus of the Great Southern & Western Railway (1846–48), by Sancton Wood, reputedly modelled on Inigo Jones's Banqueting House in Whitehall, in 1991 (Author)

Fig 5.5 Dartford Station, by Samuel Beazley (1849), in 1967. The first floor extension and wooden building on the left were later additions. The entire station has since been replaced (Author)

Fig 5.6 The original station at Newmarket in 1955, now demolished (R.E.G.Read/Author)

Several architects worked with, or for, Robert Stephenson. Although he was an architect by profession, John Livock was a resident engineer on the LBR where he designed highly acclaimed stations on the Northampton to Peterborough line, and on the Trent Valley Railway, followed by the hotel that fronted Birmingham New Street Station. He was also associated with the LNWR's southern division resident engineer Robert Dockray on the Bletchley–Oxford line, and perhaps on others of the 1845–55 period (Biddle 1993, pp.61–71). There is more scope for research here.

On Stephenson's North Midland Railway of 1840, exquisite stations were built by Francis Thompson. Then he worked on the Eastern Counties between Newport, Cambridge and Brandon (1845), another Stephenson line, although two other men were also involved: Sancton Wood and Henry Hunt (Chadwick 1985). Wood was the salaried architect of the company, and Oliver Carter concludes that Thompson, and perhaps Hunt, succeeded him although there is some curious overlapping of dates (Carter 1995). A year later Thompson was working on the Chester & Holyhead, where he designed a notable series of stations, as well as his work on Stephenson's two tubular bridges.

He has also been credited with the iron trainsheds at Derby and Chester, where he designed the handsome station buildings. This seems unlikely, as a solo job; Stephenson, as engineer, would undoubtedly have had overall control, while at Chester, *Parry's Railway Companion from Chester to Holyhead* (1849) credits the roof to Charles H. Wild, one of Stephenson's assistants. It would be interesting to know whether the drawings are signed, although the value of a signature can be questioned. It has been stated that it does not 'signify authorship or inspiration' (Haworth 1994, p.69), which sprang from the signatory's superior, although today and for long past it has been the practice for the superior to sign drawings as an acknowledgement of approval of the designs by the man at the drawing board. Again, more hard evidence is needed in order to form a judgement.

The same applies to Stephenson's relationship with two other men: Charles Fox and John Dobson. Fox was a pupil appointed by Stephenson as resident engineer on the southern end of the LBR, and with whom he designed the pioneer light iron roofs for Euston and Birmingham Curzon Street, a basic form which Stephenson and others thereafter used countless times at home and overseas, and which on the LNWR became almost standard. Fox went on to become one of the foremost structural engineers of his day and a partner in the well known firm of Fox Henderson & Co. In 1904 his son, Francis, claimed that his father 'designed the present roof over the Euston station, the first of the kind ever made' (Fox 1904, p.4). But as he goes on to say that his father 'designed or built' the roofs at Birmingham New Street, Paddington, Waterloo and York, his ground may be shaky, for we know that although they were erected by Fox Henderson, the designers were others, except for New Street which was the work of E.A. Cowper on Fox Hendersons' staff. When we consider the enormous pressure that Stephenson was under on the LBR, it seems more likely that he quickly sketched out an idea for the Euston roof, or even did it verbally, and instructed Fox, in whom he seems to have had implicit trust, to get on with it.

Stephenson's relationship with Dobson is more difficult. Dobson was a Newcastle architect of standing and distinction; a designer of many notable houses, churches and public buildings; some docks, warehouses and bridges; and some railway works. Not all were built, but his reputation and his completed output were formidable. His greatest existing achievement is Newcastle Central Station, despite the original design having been modified by his successor. Stephenson was the engineer and Dobson's name has been joined with his as designer of the Newcastle High Level Bridge and the great arched iron roof of the station, the first to be built on a curve. Stephenson, at a dinner given in his honour, disclaimed anything more than 'drawing the outline' of the roof, giving credit 'for the execution' to his resident engineer T.E. Harrison. But Dobson, in his presidential address to the Northern Architectural Association in 1859, nine years afterwards, said that he 'originate[d] a new style of roofing at the Central Station, Newcastle... by introducing curved principals.' (Wilkes 1980, Appendix 1, p.109). Why would he claim credit for something he did not do when his professional standing was so widely recognized? He went on to say that they were produced 'by a simple contrivance of bevelled rollers'; not, be it noted, that he designed the rollers himself, as has often been stated. Wrought iron was, in fact, rolled in curved sections as early as 1820 (Paxton 1990, p.119). Dobson himself does not, however, make any claim on the High Level Bridge. That appeared in the list of his works prepared by his daughter in 1885, as amended by Wilkes, but would seem unlikely.

As we have seen, in the early years there was no clear distinction between architects, engineers, and surveyors; it was not until the mid nineteenth century that quite separate professions began to form. The rivalry between engineers and architects in late Victorian times and since is well known. Now it has largely been superseded by the multidisciplinary teamwork needed in designing large, complex modern buildings, and many leading architects, like Richard Rogers and Nicholas Grimshaw (who designed the spectacular new roof at Waterloo International) are also skilled in structural engineering. F.R. Conder (Conder 1983, p.83) sets out the relationship in the early days between a chief engineer and his resident 'who did the main part of the work, while the other [the chief] obtained the lion's share of the credit and pay.' Unfortunately he has been misquoted, out of context, on the relationship between engineer and architect, creating further misunderstanding (Haworth 1994, p.69 n.246). The answer must surely be that in practice they all worked together, with or without harmony. These structures could only have been produced by close collaboration, which is what they were paid for.

There are other railway architects about whom one would like to know more, particularly their terms of employment and by whom they were engaged. That undercapitalised company, the South Eastern Railway, employed Samuel Beazley from about 1847 to 1851 for its London Bridge terminus, stations on the North Kent line, and houses at Ashford. He was best known for the colonnade at Drury Lane Theatre. The South Eastern hitherto had mainly gone in for cheap, wooden stations, so why the sudden change? Beazley was followed by William Tress until 1855, and he designed some excellent, but expensive, stations between Tunbridge Wells and Hastings. He was also the company's surveyor and valuer, responsible for purchasing land, as indeed Beazley may have been.

Again, Tite was not the only architect who was also a railway director. Tress, David Mocatta and Sancton Wood were directors of the Reading Guildford & Reigate Railway, which became part of the South Eastern. Edwin Course says he is satisfied that Tress designed the stations between Ash and Gomshall, and Wood the others (Course 1987). Wood is another whose life would certainly repay research. As well as his exact role on the Eastern Counties, and whether he or Thompson originated the style Thompson used so effectively on the Chester & Holyhead, we need to know what he was doing on the Rugby–Peterborough line of the LNWR where the stations at best were nondescript, apart from Luffenham which was in the Wood or Thompson manner and ascribed to Thompson (Carter 1995). Wood turns up again in Ireland, where he built a splendid series of stations on the Great Southern & Western's main line, including the Kingsbridge (now Heuston) terminus at Dublin: one of the finest stations in the British Isles.

Andrew Heiton of Perth, a wide ranging architectural practitioner, built stations for the Perth & Dunkeld, Scottish North Eastern and Edinburgh & Glasgow Railways, and Perth Station Hotel. On the last line the engineer was John Miller, who himself built superbly on the Glasgow & South Western main line, and others in central Scotland. He has been described as a competent architect (Johnston and Hume 1979, p.161), and is thought to have designed many of the stations. His later namesake, James Miller, a leading Glasgow architect, also did much fine railway work around the turn of the century.

As well as the Eastern Counties line, Henry Hunt worked for the London Brighton & South Coast and NSR. He was primarily a surveyor, but worked for the NSR as an architect, designing many of the excellent early stations and the very fine frontage building, company headquarters, houses, and hotel which form such a notable group at Stoke. He is known as 'the father of quantity surveying', having taken off the quantities for Sir Charles Barry's new Houses of Parliament single handed. He later became surveyor to H.M. Office of Works, and was knighted (Chadwick 1985). The railway work of all four deserves more investigation.

Although many architects worked for railways on a contract or retainer basis, as time went on some of the larger companies appointed them as full time salaried officials, generally in the engineer's department but later as chief officers in their own right. One of the first appears to be Charles Trubshaw, who worked in the LNWR engineer's department from 1864 to 1874, when he was appointed architect for the Midland Railway's northern division. He worked with J.H. Sanders who had been architect for the whole line but now reduced his commitment to the southern division. The Midland built very good stations, and Sanders may well have developed the distinctive and long-lived single storey 'pavilion' design which appeared all over the system. He was also responsible for the classical Bath Green Park Station of 1870. Trubshaw designed most of the later Midland stations up to his retirement in 1905, including Leicester London Road and Sheffield. He originated the company's familiar use of terracotta decoration, and his triumph was the Midland Hotel at Manchester. He is a railway architect who has, unusually, received some welcome recent attention (Dixey 1994).

Such men came to have their own departments, and as full–timers Sanders and Trubshaw pre-dated William Bell on the NER (1877–1914), who previously has been regarded as probably the first. The free hand given to men like Trubshaw and Bell indicates the high regard in which they were held. Henry Shelmerdine of the L&YR for instance, was also the company's land agent, and in 1882 at the age of 27 was earning twice as much as the chief engineer, which must have caused some ripples (*Builder* 1935).

These, then, are a few of those who are known, and further evidence continues to appear. The writer has, for instance, lately discovered (in the negative sense) that Livock did not design Buckingham station. It was not, as was thought, one of the originals on the line, but a replacement for an earlier temporary, wooden one. The evidence came from a totally unexpected source and has prompted further research. More positively, a guess that Penson's relationship with Robertson may have extended to designing the Shrewsbury & Hereford Railway stations has been borne out in the case of Hereford itself, from a contemporary newspaper account (Biddle 1993, p.141).

There are countless stations whose designers are still unknown. Who, for instance, was responsible for that remarkable series of half-timbered stations between Bletchley and Bedford, at the behest of the Duke of Bedford? It could have been the engineer, inspired by some of the 'picturesque' designs found in contemporary builders' and architects' pattern books, such as J.C. Loudon's *Encyclopaedia of Cottage, Farm and Villa Architecture* (1842). It is fairly certain that many of the decorative bargeboards, awning valances and other features of Victorian stations came from these sources, just as much of the ironwork came from ironfounders' pattern books. But that does not explain why and by whom the exquisitely delicate terminus of the little Newmarket & Chesterford Railway was designed – now, sadly, gone; Christian Barman's 'baroque orangery' (Barman, 1950 p.85); or the hugely Jacobean Maldon East, where we know the reason for its size and magnificence, but not the architect.

Might-have-beens can throw up questions, too. In the Royal Institute of British Architects' drawings collection, for instance, there are some station designs; although not many, they are of great interest. Here are four of them. John Clayton's elevation of 1856 for a Hereford central station is curious, because by then Penson had already been commissioned. And why did Clayton, a Hereford architect, in 1858 enter a competition for a new station at Glasgow Buchanan Street of all places? No doubt it was advertized in professional journals. He must have fancied his chance and did indeed win third prize. He was one of 63 entrants, none of whose designs were accepted. The Caledonian Railway balked at the cost and instead gave the job to its engineer, who produced a wooden building that remained the poor relation among Glasgow's termini until it was closed in 1968.

Dobson, too, turns up in the RIBA collection, with an elaborate Tudor terminus in the collegiate manner for the Newcastle & Carlisle Railway (NCR), 1841. Wilkes says it was for Carlisle, which would seem strange when one considers that all the other NCR stations were designed by Benjamin Green, also of Newcastle. It was more probably intended either for the central 'union' station for all the railways serving Newcastle proposed by Richard Grainger about that time, or even more likely the NCR's own station authorized for a site at the Spital, but not built. An Italianate building with twin towers and pantiled roofs was designed by Sir Charles Barry for Trentham, matching his new mansion for the Duke of Sutherland. It is a larger and more elaborate version of the station that was eventually built. The Duke paid for it, and presumably made Barry severely modify his design.

From all of the foregoing it will be evident that there is a lot to be found out, and it is hoped that this will encourage research. But how can it serve to 'demonstrate ways in which historical analysis can inform debate on current issues of railway policy', one of the other objects of the original seminar at which this paper was given? The author suggests that a better knowledge of the past can stimulate work done today and in the future, by encouraging more sensitive restoration or maintenance of historic structures. Works that have previously been disregarded may be found to be important, and the statutory listing process can be based on more accurate information than has sometimes applied in the past. The listing of railway structures itself needs reviewing on a national basis (with due regard to local interests, of course) instead of relying on the somewhat haphazard selections hitherto, weeding out unworthy or duplicated structures and adding important ones that have been missed. Work is now beginning, but such an assessment can only be made against a background that has been properly researched.

Before its demise, British Rail, aided by the Railway Heritage Trust, was alive to the importance of its 'heritage', to use that overworked word, and carried out some excellent restoration, as have many preserved railways, organisations and individuals. Railtrack's policy is now emerging with very commendable signs, but all these bodies need sound historical data as a basis for their work.

In conclusion Professor Howard Newby's article 'Into the Future' in the Spring 1995 number of the National Trust Magazine contains a very appropriate message: look outwards.

Chapter Six

The Railway in Industry

M. J. T. Lewis

The history of the industrial railway naturally divides itself into two broad periods, markedly distinct yet bound by a strong continuity. The first period is that before the Railway Age – before, let us say, 1830 – when virtually every railway was built for a purely industrial purpose. The second embraces the Railway Age and beyond, when the industrial railway continued to serve exactly the same function, but no longer stood alone. There has long been a tendency, except among the relatively small band of its devotees, to dismiss the industrial railway as something of a poor relation of the public passenger railway: at first as the uncouth and primitive caveman contrasted with his cultured and technically advanced descendants, later as the humble artisan cousin of the urbane tycoon of big business. Such a view lacks historical balance. Uncouth or humble though industrial lines might be, they played as essential a part in the evolution and flowering of the railway as cavemen and artisans did in the case of humanity.

Before the Railway Age

The formative period has been labelled the 'prehistory of railways' (Elton 1963). Not only is this title misleading, because by definition prehistory means a time before written records begin, but it also reflects the blinkered philosophy that railway history is nothing but the history of the public passenger railway from 1830. In reality the L&M did not spring up fully formed out of a vacuum, but was the first climax of a long history, the inheritor of at least two centuries of evolution, during which the ingredients of the public railway, the building blocks of most of what was to come, were assembled together.

The only tenable definition of a railway seems to be 'a prepared track which so guides the vehicles running on it that they cannot leave the track,' or words to that effect. On this basis, it is now becoming clear, the earliest true railways can be found among the rutways of classical antiquity. The famous, if misunderstood, Diolkos of Corinth, far from serving merely as a portage for ships, very probably carried goods in wagons guided by its stone rails and functioned just like a railway of a very much later date (Cook 1979; MacDonald 1986, although they do not discuss it in quite those terms). Grooves cut in the

floor of a level in a Roman gold mine in Portugal imply railway transport of a
type that ultimately became commonplace in such circumstances (Wahl 1993).
There is no doubt at all that, on the above definition, underground railways
aplenty existed during the late Middle Ages and Renaissance in the metal mines
of continental Europe, and that in the 1560s they came to Britain (to the Mines
Royal in Cumberland and perhaps, later, in Wales). Nor is there any doubt that
they played a major role in carrying ore and waste from the working face to the
shaft or adit mouth. The method of guidance varied. Sometimes, and perhaps
originally, it was grooved wooden rails, sometimes it was guide wheels, most
commonly it was a pin between the rails. Although their vehicles were mostly
small and were pushed by hand, and although their forms of guidance ultimately
(but only in the present century) proved to be evolutionary cul-de-sacs, these
lines were still railways.

It would be extremely interesting to know whether there was any continuity
between the rutways of Roman mines and the grooved wooden tracks of late
medieval ones. If there was, the evidence is best sought in Byzantine mines of
Asia Minor or the Balkans, for it was in the Eastern Empire rather than in
western Europe that Roman technology tended to survive. The search in this
largely unexplored subject area would be a specialist and difficult one, and a
long shot; but it deserves to be tried. Nor, one may be sure, has the last word
been said about the primitive railways of continental metal mines, let alone of
the British ones of this early phase, nor about the influence (if any) that they
may have exerted on later developments.

Almost all of the main stream of early railway development, however, took
place in the coal industry in Britain. Here, the first known surface railway was
built at Wollaton near Nottingham in 1603–4; by 1605 it was to be found in
Shropshire and by 1608 in Northumberland. From the start, in all probability, its
wagons were guided by flanged wheels, which were certainly standard in Britain
well before the century was out. This was the direct ancestor of all that was to
come. As part and parcel of a colliery's equipment, it was privately owned. It
therefore had but a single user and its traffic was essentially one way. It was
short in length, the track was of wood, the motive power was the horse, but it
was a railway, recognizable as such to modern eyes had they been there to see.
It is not categorically certain that the Wollaton railway really was the first. We
should not close our eyes to the possibility that it had predecessors (most likely
in Shropshire) of which we have not yet found the record, and deeper delving in
the archives may yet spring some surprises. What is certain is that in this form
the railway throve, at first almost exclusively in the coal industry whose
transport problems it had been invented to solve. Its twin centres of
development, from where its technology spread to other areas, were the
Tyneside and the Shropshire coalfields, each of which evolved distinctive
technical details. It remained short: for a couple of centuries few lines measured

more than a dozen miles, running down to (usually) the sea or to the nearest navigable river, after which the coal continued its journey by water. On the most important lines, traffic could be heavy: in 1727 the great Tanfield way in Durham carried nearly half a million tons and on average 930 loaded wagons passed down it every day.

During the eighteenth century the railway also found its way underground in coal mines where, though necessarily small in size, it spread over a considerable mileage; but details of its history, form and extent are still surprisingly nebulous. The railway was also adopted by the iron industry and, less commonly, by metal mines and by quarries. To many industries which handled bulk commodities the railway was already proving itself indispensable, and without the railway the Great Northern coalfield or the Shropshire iron industry, to take the most obvious examples, could hardly have maintained their earlier output, let alone burgeoned in the way they did.

As the second half of the eighteenth century progressed, the original and limited concept of the railway became more complex, and some merging of regional differences took place. Some of the features of the expanding canal network – its multiple user principle, its revolutionary civil engineering and its ability to carry goods over long distances – came gradually to be applied to railways too. Many railways were built as extensions of canals or as feeders to them, often by other parties, but sometimes by the canal companies themselves. Hence the principle of the common carrier began, tentatively at first, to be transferred to the railway. Perhaps the first manifestation of this, at least in theory, was on the TMC's Caldon Low railway, opened in probably 1773; but it was not until the 1790s that canal owned railways proliferated, on which tolls were charged just as on the canals themselves. Early examples are the Little Eaton Gangway near Derby, the Loughborough & Nanpantan Railway, and a growing number of lines in South Wales, most notably those of the Monmouthshire Canal. From here it was but a short step to the independent railway company, usually incorporated by act of parliament, whose line was almost by definition a public one, although it still, in nearly every case, had an industrial *raison d'être* behind it. The Surrey Iron Railway's act of 1801, the first of this kind, was followed before 1830 by nearly forty more.

Public railways were often longer than their private counterparts; the combined length of the Hay and Kington Railways of 1816–20, for instance, was 36 miles, and two way traffic became commonplace, with regular passenger services occasionally being provided. Passengers, indeed, were probably carried informally and unofficially on more lines than we imagine (Kidner 1994). Of equal importance, on the technical front, from the 1790s the cast iron rail began to replace the wooden, and two decades later the wrought iron rail began to take the place of cast iron; from 1803 experiments were made with locomotives instead of horses; tunnels, earthworks and bridges now existed of fair size and in fair numbers; simple signalling arrangements were employed, if not commonly; and the train appeared, in the sense of a string of vehicles rather than wagons in ones or twos. Almost all the basic ingredients of the fully fledged railway were in place well before the L&M. Early railways, then, hand in hand with the canals, laid the conceptual and technical foundations on which the Railway Age was built, and played a role of vital importance to subsequent history.

Having set the scene, let us turn to a brief survey of recent work and of the areas where further research is needed. The long period starting about 1600 is most conveniently divided into two parts: before and after the coming of the iron rail. Over twenty-five years ago I attempted to establish the framework of the development of wooden railways (Lewis 1970). The canvas I had to paint was very large; possibly too large, since it extended from Ireland to Central Asia and from the fifteenth century to roughly 1800. Though building on the work of previous writers, my work broke new ground, and I did not and do not fool myself that I said everything that could be said, or that what I did say was infallible. I hoped, rather, to provide a basis for further research. In the event, the response has in general proved disappointing. It has prompted a little dotting of i's and crossing of t's and some limited reporting of lines that I had missed, but only one major new contribution (Bennett, Clavering and Rounding 1990). This invaluable work studies the wagonways of the south bank of the Tyne in the context of the byzantine politics of the local coal trade in the seventeenth and eighteenth centuries, it expands on, and sometimes corrects, my own book. It underlines the fact that (in this period as in every other) railways were not self-sufficient entities divorced from the economic and social world around them; it emphasizes the value of local expertise which the academic from afar can never acquire; and it sets an example for comparable studies for other parts of Britain. Other pointers to future work are the recent and exciting discoveries of buried stretches of wooden track at Bersham near Wrexham and at Lambton in County Durham (Grenter 1993; Nolan and Durkin 1996). Further finds of this nature will of necessity depend largely on chance, but we do now know not only that such survivals are possible but that there is a particular kind of site where we should keep our eyes open for them.

For the age of the early iron railway (1790s to, say, 1830) a very sizeable bibliography could be compiled. There are shelves full of books – usually small books – and of articles on individual tramways or on limited areas; many of them of great value in terms of detail, and all contributing to the overall picture of development. The Railway & Canal Historical Society has a Tramroad Group dedicated to the study of all railways of this early type (without, wisely, defining the term too closely), which at the time of writing has produced no less than 115 Occasional Papers for limited circulation. South Wales has received more attention than any other region. To impart some idea of the literature becoming available and to underline the contribution that individuals can make, let us list (from selected journals only, and omitting the many relevant Occasional Papers just mentioned) the books and articles published since 1975 which relate specifically to South Wales tramroads: Cook and Clinker 1984; Hughes 1990; Lewis 1975; Rattenbury 1980, 1982, 1983, 1988, 1989; Rattenbury and Cook 1996; Reynolds 1979, 1980; Tann 1996. Most, however, deal with tramroads on the fringes of the heavily industrialized area, and even Rattenbury tended to steer clear of the valleys themselves, with their complex systems and their industrial politics just as convoluted as those of Tyneside. It will be a long time before the story of South Wales tramroads is fully told.

Elsewhere in Britain too there are many recent investigations into individual lines. Though fewer for any given area than in South Wales, and though some major regions such as Tyneside have been grievously neglected, it is impossible to cite them all. As far as they go, they are mostly admirable. Yet, with a few honourable exceptions such as Hughes (1990), whose masterly work has a scope and significance much wider than its title implies, the focus of this genre tends to be narrow, the local case study rather than the regional, let alone national, overview. It is generally easier, after all, to limit research to the neat confines of a single line than it is to compare its features with their counterparts elsewhere. While one often wishes that authors had put their particular railway into context, no serious criticism is intended. The point is that this multiplicity of relatively small scale studies underlines the lack of a good overall survey of the early iron railway. Dendy Marshall (1938) and Lee (1943), though pioneering in their day, are by now thoroughly out of date, while Baxter (1966), who attempted to fill the gap, did not fill it well. Daunting though the task would be, the field is wide open for an authoritative study of the crucial thirty or forty years which led up to the Railway Age and made it possible.

While such a book with a national coverage is devoutly to be desired, there is still plenty of room for regional studies; a book – equally in need of writing – entitled *The Tyneside Wagonway 1790–1830* would tell a very different story from one on the South Wales tramroad over the same period. The same could be said, albeit on a slightly smaller scale, of almost every other industrial area: lowland Scotland, Lancashire, Yorkshire, the West Midlands. There is endless scope too for surveys of railways in particular industries or in parts of them: in coal mines underground, in coal mines on the surface, in metal mines, in ironworks, in slate quarries.

In addition to national or regional surveys, all manner of thematic problems cry out for investigation. One of the most crucial issues concerns that most fundamental part of any railway, the permanent way. This was a time of rapid change in the iron industry, when cast iron was simultaneously being adopted for bridges and for the internal framing of industrial buildings, and its structural properties were becoming understood. Although the broad outline of the evolution of cast and wrought iron rail is known, it still enshrines a good measure of myth, and there was very considerable regional variation and very rapid improvement in design. Detailed regional typologies need to be established, for which coordinated fieldwork is the best tool. The volume of material available is huge if intractable. Of contemporary publications, some of the less accessible are now easily available (e.g., von Oeynhausen and von Dechen 1971); of the scattered mass of records of industrial concerns, iron founders and engineers, only a few (but very useful) extracts and distillations have appeared (e.g., Riden 1973; Skempton and Andrews 1976–77; Hadfield and Skempton 1979); and large numbers of actual specimens languish untapped in museums or await discovery in the field.

Then there is that curious interlude of the plate rail, invented by John Curr of Sheffield and disseminated in the 1790s by Benjamin Outram of Butterley Ironworks and others. So successful was it that, despite its structural and practical drawbacks, it threatened for a while to drive the edge rail out of existence; had it done so, the subsequent course of railway history might have been very different. Why and how did this state of affairs come about? Was it deficiencies in the current design of iron edge rails? Was it high pressure salesmanship by Outram and his colleagues? Was it railway owners jumping blindly on the bandwagon of fashion? It is an issue which nobody has seriously addressed; yet it is an important issue, for the plate rail, in hindsight, was an aberration from the main stream of evolution more significant than the atmospheric railway or even perhaps than the broad gauge. It is for reasons of this sort that early railways deserve to be studied not, so to speak, as an optional module, but as an integral part of the core course of railway history.

Still in the technical field, we are badly in need of an authoritative history of the early locomotive. This made its first tentative appearance in 1803 as a purely experimental variation on the new theme of the high pressure steam engine, and only began to achieve viability and national fame with Blenkinsop and Murray's Middleton engines of 1812. Such a history should continue at least to 1830 when the *Planet* inaugurated a new era, and even, in respect of survivals of old style locomotive engineering, to a later date still – one thinks of the products of Hackworth or the Neath Abbey Ironworks in the 1830s. Since the last general survey appeared (Dendy Marshall 1953) a great deal of new information has come to light, some of it published (e.g., Lewis 1975; Weaver 1983; Mulholland 1978), most of it still lurking in archives. One promising avenue is the impressive research currently under way at Beamish Museum on the spate of activity on Tyneside from 1813 by Chapman, Buddle, Hedley and Stephenson. And, to turn to economic as opposed to technical questions, to what extent was the development of the locomotive stimulated by such factors as the rising price of horses and of their fodder during the Napoleonic wars, a stimulus often cited but barely investigated?

Along with the Newcomen engine for pumping, the railway had permitted the expansion of the coal industry which otherwise, without adequate transport, might actually have contracted; to what other industries might the same apply? This sort of question has much to do with economic considerations about the availability of capital which industrialists needed to invest in railways before their industry could expand. It also has much to do with geographical considerations about the availability, or impossibility, of other forms of transport: one thinks of the ironworks of the South Wales valleys, or the slate quarries of the North Wales mountains, where canals could never be practical and roads could never be adequate. A striking instance is the line serving the Penrhyn Quarry near Bangor, surveyed as a canal by Thomas Dadford in 1799, rejected as impracticable, re-surveyed by him as a railway in 1800 and built, though not exactly to his specification, in 1801. Within ten years it was reported that

> the original expense of construction, the interest of the sum expended, the wear and tear of iron work, carriages, etc., etc., have been amply repaid and recompensed by the diminution of breakage among the slates, the prodigious extension of their sale, and above all (in a public point of view) by the reduced number of horses, an animal which like the sheep has become more oppressively consuming than a wolf. Heretofore the slates were carried first in panniers and subsequently in carts, which, 140 in number, took an equal number of oxen and no less than 400 horses from the pursuits of agriculture. The business is now done upon its very extended scale by sixteen horses and twelve men and boys. The improvement of the agriculture of the parish has been strikingly conspicuous (Hall 1952, p.105).

The railway reduced the cost of transport to a fifth of its former level. How typical is this example of a direct linkage between the acquisition of cheap and reliable rail transport and an increase in output or in profitability?

Again, how much did early railways owe to canals in terms of engineering? The Dadfords and some of their colleagues spring to mind as builders of both; but then South Wales, their stamping ground, whatever its mileage of tramroad, was not for long in the van of technical progress. How and where did other early railway engineers learn their trade? On Tyneside and, to a lesser degree, in lesser coalfields they were heirs to a long tradition, and such men from the established centres of railways were in great demand elsewhere. In more marginal areas, however, it seems that sometimes they had no specialist training but relied on basic surveying skills and on mother wit. This was evidently the case with James Spooner, whose background was in land surveying and apparently in the Ordnance Survey, but who laid out the Ffestiniog Railway on a superb route through extremely difficult terrain (Lewis 1996). The whole matter of the transfer of engineering techniques from one sphere of transport to another, and from one region to another, is in need of investigation.

The canal system, we have seen, attracted feeder railways. Many canal acts of parliament, especially during the Canal Mania, authorized specific railways or gave blanket permission for railways to be built to the canal from works within a certain distance, usually four to eight miles. If, on application by an industrialist, the canal company refused to build such a railway, its powers to do so were transferred to the applicant. In either case the line was to be open to the public on payment of a toll. Apart from a very few early exceptions such as that at Caldon Low, one of the first of these railways was built at Merthyr Tydfil under the Glamorganshire Canal's four mile clause by the Dowlais Ironworks in 1792. This line was also remarkable in that it was apparently the first to employ cast iron rails, albeit only crude bars, which were self-contained and did not rest on wooden rails for strength (Lewis 1975). The Dowlais Railway was closely followed in 1792–94 by a series of lines – including the Rassa, Beaufort and Blaenafon – feeding from various ironworks to the Monmouthshire Canal and by the Clydach Railroad feeding to the Brecknock & Abergavenny Canal. All were built by the canal companies under their respective acts and were therefore public. All were engineered by members of the Dadford family and had a gauge of 3ft 4in and rails – all too liable to break under traffic – only slightly stronger than those at Dowlais (Hadfield 1960; Rattenbury 1980).

In 1797, after several years' gestation, another local Dadford line, the Trevil Railroad, was opened. This was different in that it was built not by the canal company but by a partnership of ironmasters, the Trevil Rail Road Company (Hadfield 1960); but because it was authorized by the Monmouthshire Canal's eight mile clause it was public. Next year, near Wakefield, there appeared the Lake Lock Railroad. While the engineer was a local man, Israel Rhodes, its rails resembled the Dadford type and its gauge was the Dadfords' 3ft 4in, although the nature of Rhodes' link with Wales is unknown. Like Trevil, it was another public line built by its own company, but it was different again (and very unusual) in that the necessary land was allotted to it by the enclosure commissioners with the avowed purpose of removing 'the heavy Carriage of Coal' from the roads. It has some claim to be the first public railway not authorized by a canal act (Goodchild 1977). It is easy to see how the next step came about: the public railway which, in the absence of canals or of accommodating enclosure commissioners, needed compulsory purchase powers granted directly by parliament. The first such, as we have seen, was the Surrey Iron Railway Act of 1801. This sequence of events, besides illustrating something of the transfer of technology, also summarizes the early evolution of the concept of the public railway. But only as we understand it: the question is whether our understanding, which is undoubtedly incomplete, is broadly correct.

In the beginning of the nineteenth century a few far sighted men canvassed the potential of a national system of railways. One such was Sir Richard Phillips, whose classic musings are short enough to quote. A visit to the Surrey Iron Railway, which some envisaged as the first link in a chain of railways to connect London with Portsmouth, prompted him to write:

> I found renewed delight on witnessing, at this place, the economy of horse labour on the Iron Railway. Yet a heavy sigh escaped me, as I thought of the inconceivable millions which have been spent about *Malta*, four or five of which might have been the means of extending *double lines of iron railway* from London to Edinburgh, Glasgow, Holyhead, Milford, Falmouth, Yarmouth, Dover, and Portsmouth! A reward of a single thousand would have supplied coaches and other vehicles, of various degrees of speed, with the best tackle for readily turning out; and we might, ere this, have witnessed our mail coaches running at the rate of ten miles an hour, drawn by a single horse, *or impelled 15 miles an hour by Blenkinsop's steam engine*. Such would have been a legitimate motive for overstepping the income of a nation; and the completion of so great and useful a work would have afforded rational ground for public triumph in general jubilees! (Phillips 1814)

Similarly pioneering visionaries were James Anderson (1801, pp.198–217), Richard Lovell Edgeworth (1813), Thomas Gray (1820) and William James (Payne 1961). In their day they were prophets without much honour, but ultimately their visions became reality. To what extent were they responsible for preparing public opinion to accept a system of public railways?

The list of such questions in need of answers could be extended almost indefinitely; but the two points have perhaps been made. First, to ignore the formative period is like a historian of steam power beginning with Watt and ignoring Newcomen. Second, there is still an almost limitless amount of work to be done on the formative period, and important work at that.

During the Railway Age

After 1830 the private industrial railway continued, in essence, precisely as before. That it was no longer the only kind of railway did not mean that its importance was thereby diminished. Quite the reverse: it blossomed where it had blossomed before – notably in the colliery, the ironworks and the quarry. In addition it came to flourish in every other industrial situation imaginable: engineering workshops, railway works, motor works, shipyards, docks, military depots, gasworks, sewage works, waterworks, power stations, peat bogs, clay pits, agriculture, forestry; in the construction of railways, roads, dams, harbour works, airfields, and so on. It continued in the form of the internal system, often of narrow gauge, carrying coal underground from the face to the shaft, iron ore from the mine to the furnace, pig iron from foundry to forge, waste to the quarry tips, finished products from factory to warehouse. It continued, most commonly on the standard gauge, as the external link to the port or canal or – now – to the main line railway. It remained private, carrying only the owner's traffic. Technically it may often have been simple and inglorious, but it was an indispensable part of the infrastructure of industry, on a par with the colliery's pumping engine, the ironworks' furnace or the gasworks' retorts. As such, it is fodder for the historian of industry, whether general or particular. But it is also a railway, and as such it has as great a claim as any other kind of railway to the attention of the serious railway historian.

Nobody concerned with railway history is unaware of the existence of these industrial railways. Too few historians take them seriously, too many disdain them as peripheral and trivial. It is perfectly true that (to coin an example) Joe Bloggs' scrapyard in Bristol, served by a 300 yard branch up which an aged Manning Wardle pottered twice a week is, taken by itself, very small beer indeed when set against the power and the glory of the Great Western Railway. But what about the railways of the Port of London Authority, with a hundred locomotives and several hundred miles of track, a system quite as complex as that of many a pre-grouping main line company (Peacock 1952)? Or the Round Oak steelworks in the Black Country, by no means the largest in Britain, which in 1876 already had 40 miles of track and first and last owned 63 locomotives (Gale 1975)? A large slate quarry in Wales could boast a hundred miles of tramway, and even in these degenerate days British Steel at Scunthorpe still has 115 miles. Nor is it widely appreciated how astonishingly numerous and ubiquitous these industrial railways were. Two examples from the Industrial Railway Society's handbooks may illustrate the point. In the historical county of Durham (but excluding Teesside) there have been something like 500 locations with privately owned locomotive operated railways (Mountford and Charlton 1977); the figure is approximate simply because of the difficulty of defining separate locations. In the county of Dyfed, larger in area but hardly a hive of industry, there have been 101 such locations (de Havilland 1994). These figures, moreover, ignore the large number of railways which never had locomotives at all. Taken *en masse*, industrial railways were very far from despicable.

To establish the total mileage of them in Britain, even to a first approximation, would be a major research undertaking in its own right, and I can attempt here only the roughest of guesses. A good proportion of the locations in County Durham were collieries and ironworks which would each have scores of miles of track and, including the underground lines in the mines, a fair number would reach 100 miles. On this sort of basis it seems that, first and last and in the roundest of figures, the 500 locations in Durham would have totalled at least 5,000 miles of railway. Multiply that figure by a modest factor of ten for the whole of Britain, and the result is a good 50,000 miles, which my instinct says is a considerable underestimate. But this total is the same as the total track mileage (not route mileage), including sidings, owned by all the public railways of Britain when at their maximum extent. Traffic, too, was large. For some years after 1910, for instance, the single firm of Lambton, Hetton & Joicey Collieries Ltd raised an annual average of four million tons of coal, all of which would travel both on its underground and on its surface railways. Of all the goods carried by the public railways, with the major exception of agricultural produce, a high proportion originated from, or ended on, industrial railways, and would often traverse their metals more than once in the form of raw materials in and finished products out. There were also concerns, many and large (especially coal mines in the North East, and quarries within reach of the coast), which sent their produce straight to the quay on their own railways, without patronizing the main line companies at all. It is entirely possible that industrial railways carried a greater annual tonnage than the public railways did; although if reckoned in ton-miles the total, in the nature of things, was doubtless smaller.

My purpose in bandying these figures and these guesses is in no sense to weigh the two kinds of railway against each other, but rather to offer some kind of yardstick, however crude, by which the extent of industrial railways may be gauged. Taken together, they were very big business indeed; and for that reason alone they deserve much more attention than most railway historians allow them. Heretical though it might sound, it could plausibly be argued that the industrial, economic, social and even physical shaping of County Durham owed just as much to industrial railways as to the North Eastern Railway itself. Obviously there were differences. The NER was a unity and was big business in its own right; though independent, it was a component of the nation-wide network, it was party to the Railway Clearing House and to inter company agreements, it was subject to a succession of general railway acts of parliament. The railways of the Pontop Hall Colliery or of Hawks Crawshay & Co, engineers of Gateshead, were not; they were disparate, smaller, individualistic, and hard to generalize about. Their records, if they survive at all, are scattered, not neatly assembled on the shelves at Kew or within the covers of the Blue Books or the *Railway Year Book*; they did not feature, or barely, in the contemporary railway press, and they have no handy Tomlinson or Hoole for the historian to consult. The history of industrial railways is not easy to research.

They had their own story, naturally related to that of the main lines, but distinct from it. Except for the relatively few cases of statutory or public railways that were essentially industrial ones, their financing was obviously quite different. Except for a few concerns that ran an internal passenger service, they carried only freight. They did not, on the whole, demand such heavy engineering works, and their architecture is rarely other than mundane. But to despise or ignore these later industrial railways as insignificant appendages to the main line system is as short sighted and, bluntly, as poor history as it is to relegate the earlier formative period to the sidelines.

This is not to say that they have been ignored. The field is led by the Industrial Railway Society which has been at work for the last fifty years, at first concentrating largely on locomotives but in recent times laudably broadening its outlook. It publishes the excellent *Industrial Railway Record* and regional handbooks, of which, in the current series, twelve volumes have so far appeared, with still a long way to go. These handbooks are works of astonishing virtuosity. Although their prime purpose is to focus quite narrowly on locomotives, they provide an outline history of each owning company. These entries encapsulate a prodigious amount of industrial and business history, and they offer an invaluable starting point for the researcher who wishes to use a wide-angle lens.

There are, too, plenty of books and a plethora of articles on relatively narrow aspects of the subject, such as the individual railway, the railways of a limited area, or the products of a particular locomotive builder. Restricting ourselves to books, the standpoint from which they are written tends to fall into one of four categories:

1. The industrial railway as an end in itself, with little reference to its industry and to the transport pattern of its neighbourhood. Sometimes these are simply picture books, and often they concentrate on the locomotives to the exclusion of most else. Examples need not be cited.

2. The industrial railway as part of the infrastructure of an industry. A good instance is Eric Tonks' great work on the Midlands ironstone railways, which began almost as a member of Category 1, but in its revised edition has grown from 316 to 2,116 pages, and whose new title reflects its changed priorities (Tonks 1959, 1988–92). Another, much smaller in scale, is Booth (1995) on the simple privately owned coal mines of South Wales.

3. The industrial railway seen as part of the local transport scene; good examples are Hudson (1971) on Aberford, Messenger (1978) on Caradon and Looe, and the two volumes of Townley, Smith and Peden (1991–92) on the Wigan coalfield, none of which ignore Category 2 either.

4. The industrial railway in the total context of industry, society and transport. A delightful specimen is Smith (1967) on the Dalmellington ironworks.

The overall picture is thus very similar to that in the earlier period. Most of these publications are of great value, and there is plenty of room for many more of the kind. Yet this sort of material – especially in Category 1 – can be undeniably bitty and restricted in scope; it needs to be drawn together, fleshed out, and upgraded to the standards of Category 2 or 3, or even 4. Because material is more readily available, published work has also concentrated mainly on the later part of the period. We are desperately in need of broader enquiries, especially on the earlier decades, say from 1830 to 1870. There are topics galore, both general and particular, that deserve scrutiny. One first example. The conversion of gauge on the GWR in 1892 is justly famous. A comparable situation arose in 1849 in South Wales, where the Monmouthshire Railway & Canal Co had inherited 181½ miles (including private branches) of old fangled plateway feeding down to Newport. There were 23 locomotives and 4,161 wagons on it belonging to the company and to private owners, many of whom operated their own traffic over the company's metals. In 1849 the system, decrepit and inefficient, carried 714,455 tons. The company decided to drag it into the Railway Age by converting it to standard gauge edge railways, with necessarily a brand new fleet of locomotives and wagons, and with compensation payable to the private owners where appropriate (PP 1850 XXXI, Report of Commissioners of Railways, App. 74). The story of the conversion must be a fascinating one; but it has never been told (although Rattenbury 1983 and 1988 touch on it).

A few wider questions may be selected from the many that need answering. Some concern the installation of new industrial lines or their acquisition of locomotives. What factors other than a hard look at relative costings weighed with industrialists when investing in their own private railways? A rare insight, drawn from the minutes of the Works Subcommittee of Birmingham Corporation's Gas Department in the 1870s and 1880s is to be found in Shill (1989). At what stage in their careers and in what numbers did the newer industries such as gasworks and cement works join the older industries like collieries and ironworks as members of the railway club? To what extent did the epic battles over wayleaves that had characterized the Tyneside railway from its earliest days find echoes in the Victorian period? There were certainly some cases, such as the slate quarry which was refused access from one direction and had to find it in another (Lewis and Denton 1974); but how typical were they? And how and when did the necessary practical and economic relationship between industry and the main line railways develop, and how much did it vary between industries or between railway companies? This involves such matters as the provision of an infrastructure capable of handling heavy industrial traffic, junctions with industrial lines, and running powers of one's engines over the other's metals.

An instance of the potential latent in such questions may be seen in the following. When in 1845 the LBR and the GWR were competing to extend their networks through the Black Country,

> a majority of local businessmen, representing no fewer than 46 ironworks, 57 furnaces and 98 collieries, supported the London & Birmingham's proposal, and this eventually won favour with the Railways Committee ... The Board of Trade officials drew attention to the London & Birmingham

Railway's intention 'to lay down an additional double line of rails throughout the mineral district, to be devoted entirely to the accommodation of the mineral traffic.' They recognized that if the local ironworks and mines were to benefit from railways, a whole network of short branches or tramroads would have to flow out from the main lines and great care would have to be taken to prevent the local movement of wagons from interrupting the working of larger trains in and out of the area. Indeed, this was one of the major difficulties in the 1870s and 1880s; in 1881, J. Grierson, general manager of the Great Western Railway, admitted to the Select Committee that it would not be worthwhile for his company to see more coal carried between Round Oak Ironworks and Hickman's works near Deepfields on the grounds that 'it would have, and must have, the effect of blocking our main line.' It would appear that though the railway company had initially made a good case for servicing the district's needs with regard to the mineral traffic, it had failed to fulfil this aim (Le Guillou 1975, p.109).

This kind of situation deserves spelling out in greater detail; but it rarely is. A shining exception is Lodge 1994 on the Midland line between Sheffield and Barnsley and its industrial feeders.

The early development of locomotives took place, exclusively and necessarily, on industrial railways. By 1830, however, only a small minority of such lines could boast steam engines, and further development became for a time the prerogative of main line railways. True, some engine building in pre-1830 style continued in industrial areas such as South Wales to which the main line railway came quite late, but to designs which could hardly be called progressive. Otherwise for many years locomotives remained a rarity on industrial lines. In so far as they were found at all, they were main line types and often second-hand main line engines which, as tender engines, were hardly well adapted to the purpose. It was only in 1848 that tank engines were first produced, by George England and William Bridges Adams, initially for branch line work and only in 1854–55 specifically for industrial use, by Neilson of Glasgow and E. B. Wilson of Leeds. Only in the 1860s did this preliminary trickle become a flood, with the rise of such familiar firms as Manning Wardle, Hudswell Clarke, Hunslet and Bagnall. The principal upshot was the small tank engine that dominated the industrial scene thereafter as long as steam endured.

The outline story of the emergence of the industrial steam locomotive and of specialist builders is reasonably well known (e.g., Industrial Locomotive Society 1967); an excellent history of one of the pioneering firms of builders is available in Redman (1972); and the early development of the narrow gauge locomotive in the 1850s and especially the 1860s has recently been studied in some depth (Ransom 1996). Nonetheless, the story of the emergence of the standard gauge locomotive in the 1850s and of the personalities and firms behind it is still nebulous, and needs charting in considerably greater detail. Why, too, did industrial railways fight shy of locomotives for so long? Was the traffic on most lines so light that horse traction remained adequate, or was it merely that suitable engines were just not available? And when suitable engines did come to be designed, was it in response to a specific demand generated by growing traffic levels or by a need for economizing on haulage costs?

Another aspect of significance is the contractor's line: the railway to build a railway (or a reservoir, or the Manchester Ship Canal, or what have you), a practice that had been established in canal construction as far back as the 1790s. The literature on the larger contractors themselves and on their businesses is not insubstantial; but that on the countless miles of railway which they used is heavily biased towards lists of contracts and of locomotives. There are partial exceptions. Tipper (1975), for instance, deals with the railways of South Wales reservoir contracts. Rolt (1971), on the building of the Great Central's London extension, excellent though it is, is essentially based on the great Newton collection of photographs. Bennett (1927), surely one of the most delightful, if not the most accurate, railway books ever written, has in Isaac Watt Boulton and his locomotives a subject far too idiosyncratic to be typical. As far as I am aware there is no serious study available of the formidable logistics of the contractor's railway: the acquisition and delivery of huge quantities of materials to the right place, the maintenance of equipment, its storage or transfer between contracts. A comparable if lesser question is the development of the light and portable railway, widely used for constructional work, land reclamation, and quarries and mines with working faces that were constantly shifting. In its later forms (Decauville and Jubilee track) it is well enough known, but what of their antecedents? The prototype was evidently devised for Irish bogs as early as the 1770s, and occasional references are found over the next century (e.g., Mahon 1961; Andrews 1853, pp.130–2; *The Engineer* 11 July 1879, pp.31, 34); but how widespread was it?

What, too, do we know of the unsung engineers who surveyed and built industrial lines, especially in mountainous terrain where finding a route and constructing it was no bed of roses? Were they specialists or jacks of all trades? Inclined planes, for instance, had first been applied, if sparingly, in the days of wooden rail, and multiplied hugely during the nineteenth century. Main line railways, if they used them at all, rapidly tried to give them up as an impediment to traffic flow; but in the case of industries in hilly regions, or quarries with several floors to be linked together, railways could hardly be installed without them. Regional differences are plain to see: the shallow graded inclines, mostly on the standard gauge, of the Midlands and Tyneside were a far cry in terms of design and operation from the precipitous narrow gauge inclines of the Welsh mountains. Some literature of limited scope is available (e.g., Hindley 1980), but a comparative study has never been attempted.

As with the rise, so with the fall. It is well enough known why British Railways converted from steam to internal combustion. The comparable change over on industrial lines took place, overall, markedly earlier. How similar was the reasoning and the economics which lay behind it? Again, the decline of the industrial railway was rapid and startling, and had much to do with the fork-lift truck, conveyor belt and road transport; and, indeed, with industrial decline in general. In turn it had severe repercussions on the volume of goods traffic handled by the main lines. This kind of topic is rarely addressed, though Gee (1993) covers one unexpected success story of the late 1980s and early 1990s, the Trafford Park Estate Railway. The course of the decline was naturally observed as it took place (e.g., Parker 1980). It can indeed be followed with some precision from the Industrial Railway Society's lists of existing locomotives published at intervals of about three years, from the first edition of 1969 (Etherington, Excell and Tonks) to the 11th of 1996. While, as with so many of these larger aspects, part of the answer appears obvious, the reasons behind the decline still need charting.

Such examples of pertinent questions could be multiplied. The overall picture is that the later period reflects the earlier. We do have plenty of quite narrow case studies, and we do have some good accounts of the development and decline in a few particular areas and in a few particular industries. But few thematic studies have been made. Nor, and this is the most yawning gap of all, is there a good overview – or indeed any overview, other than a picture book – of industrial railways at large. It would be no easy task, but it is crying out to be written.

There are good reasons why these gaps, large and small, remain unfilled. As already remarked, industrial railways are not easy to research. They display an enormous variety, which makes generalization difficult. Their records are much more widely scattered than those of the main line companies, and are much more likely to be totally lost. It is therefore harder to establish the facts, and harder still to interpret them. Michael Robbins in a famous paper insisted that railway historians should not only answer the question 'what?' but also 'why?' (Robbins 1957). Their first duty, he said, is to get the facts right, and to present the relevant facts to the reader; their second duty is to interpret them, to explain them to the best of their ability. Robbins was of course quite correct. Nonetheless, there are obvious limitations. One can only discuss the 'why' after one has discovered the 'what'; to quote Sherlock Holmes, it is fatal to argue ahead of one's data. When looking at railways in industry, we find it difficult to run because we are still learning to walk. True, we are not starting from square one; but compared with the study of main line railways we are still at a relatively early stage of understanding. In some areas we have plenty of detail, but not much of the necessary framework on which to hang it: it is flesh without bones. This is perhaps particularly true of industrial railways since 1830. Conversely, for the days of the wooden rail, we have something of a skeleton without much flesh on it. With industrial railways the process of full chronicling and fuller interpretation can only be a laborious and gradual one. But the effort involved is worth every drop of tears and sweat.

Amateur and Professional

Because the conference which generated these papers was concerned with the future of railway historical research, a few final and very different words are perhaps called for on the potentially vexatious distinction between professional and amateur. This is a tricky area to venture into, since it is all too easy to tread on toes. The very labels are a kind of shorthand, although most will understand what they are supposed to imply. In this context, the professional is one who makes a living out of history, especially an academic or a member of the museum or, in growing numbers, the archaeological fraternity. Amateurs come in various guises; sometimes, it is true, they live up (or down) to the slightly derogatory implications of the label, sometimes – and this cannot be overemphasized – they produce profound history. It is by no means a matter of all professionals being at one end of the spectrum and all amateurs at the other: there is a continuous shading along the whole length.

An academic myself, I write as a convinced supporter of the amateur. But snootier professionals might say that while amateurs can see no further than the trees, their own job is to look at the whole wood. This ignores two facts. First, unless someone blows away the mist surrounding the individual trees, there is no wood visible for the professional to inspect; the case studies which we have mentioned, whether of an individual tramroad or of a particular class of locomotive, are raw material for wider or deeper investigations. Second, amateurs can be just as capable as professionals of seeing the whole wood. They also have the paradoxical advantage that, though usually part timers, they often have more time to go thoroughly into their subject than does the academic who is burdened by pressures and deadlines for publication. This advantage is especially valuable in research into industrial railways, whether old or new, where the sources are essentially, and the fieldwork necessarily, local rather than available in university libraries or national repositories.

Without the amateur, railway history – and industrial railway history in particular – would hardly have got off the ground. A very high proportion of all railway history, and a high proportion of good railway history, has been written by amateurs; and in the case of industrial railways there has been very little professional input indeed. Amateurs have dominated in the past, and they will dominate in the future. It is right that they should, and they are only to be applauded and encouraged. There are few serious aspects of history to which the input from amateurs is so great, and wise academics should cooperate and interact with them, just as wise professional archaeologists seek the cooperation, not the hostility, of the metal detecting fraternity.

The sad fact remains, however, that there is sometimes a mutual suspicion. Academics can be dreadfully arrogant; they can look down their long noses at amateurs and at the technology which attracts so many of them; they can write unreadable papers aimed only at fellow academics. Conversely amateurs can resent the preaching of academics and retreat into their own narrow-minded and trivial shell: enthusiasts (in the worst sense) writing only for their soul mates. In between are the pseudo-scholars, exemplified by the author of some standing whose method is reputedly to collect information on cards, shuffle them into some sort of order, and uncritically copy them out as an almost unreadable string of facts (not always correct) with little connection between them and less attempt to explain them. All these approaches are to be deplored; they miss the full potential of their subject, and they miss much of their potential audience. The position was summed up by Robbins' admirable paper, written in 1957 but still eminently relevant today, which castigated equally enthusiasts who look no further than counting rivets on tenders and academics who hide their light under the bushel of gobbledygook.

Yet at the same time both academics and amateurs can, and do, write superb railway history, at once scholarly and accessible. True scholarship, after all, should not be exclusive, and it is not the prerogative of the academic alone. Nor, to be accessible, does history have to be popular in the sense of shallow and simplistic. This raises the question of the market for which railway history is written. It is not a rarified and utterly technical field like particle physics or the theology of the Great Schism, but one where, for inscrutable reasons, the interested public is large and informed. This public deserves to be well served, whether by professionals or by amateurs.

All this having been said, the fact remains that any hard distinction between amateurs and professionals is largely meaningless. One could name towering amateur figures who write history worthy of the best professional. Neither breed has a monopoly of intelligence, diligence, depth of knowledge or breadth of vision. The only practical difference is a superficial one: while amateurs work because it is their pleasure, professionals do so because it is their job; if it is their pleasure too, so much the better. The future of railway research lies in the hands of both. Who does it is less important than that it is done well. To do it well demands a rigorous and scholarly approach. Outside universities, this cannot be dictated in any draconian way, any more than topics for research can be allocated. Discouraging the bad and encouraging the good is a matter of publishers and journal editors thinking harder about what is needed, and being more demanding over the quality of books and articles that they accept. It is a matter of reviewers being more critical of poor publications. It is a matter of helping and encouraging, as the Railway & Canal Historical Society, for example, already does with its own publications, offering courses on how to write history, and assistance from a research index and research officer. It is a matter of education (in the best sense) through such media as the Institute of Railway Studies, adult education classes, and local and specialist societies. It is a matter of the reading public demanding high quality work on worthwhile topics. Above all, it is a matter of professional and amateur cooperating with each other and improving standards by their own good example. Michael Robbins' summary answer to his question 'What kind of railway history do we want?' was 'accurate, comprehensive, and readable.' To me, that still holds true, whoever writes it.

Chapter Seven

Technical Change and Railway Systems

Colin Divall

Such has been the intensity and longevity of interest in the technical side of Britain's railways that we might be forgiven for thinking that little remains to be written on the subject. Indeed recent reviews of transport history have not identified technical change as a priority for further work (Gourvish 1993; Robbins 1991). But the impression that the subject is in good shape is not altogether sound. While there has been a good deal of improvement in recent years with the new wave of railway historiography in periodicals such as *Backtrack,* many books and articles aimed chiefly at a lay audience still tend to be written with slight regard for the wider social, economic, political and environmental contexts of technical developments (Divall 1996). A grasp of technical detail in some degree is essential if we are to appreciate the wider significance of technical change, but we should not allow the tail to wag the dog if we want the history we write to be taken seriously by others – including those responsible for funding research – who do not share our interest in railways *per se.*

Although they are prone to other faults academics are on the whole better at the necessary contextualisation. Over the past three decades economic historians in particular have studied technical change on the American railroads of this and the last century, gaining insights into theoretical issues of general concern such as the genesis and rate of diffusion of new technologies and the effect they had on productivity. Much of this work is relevant to the historical analysis of Britain's railways.

If matters such as these are to help guide us in developing a new research agenda for the history of technical change on Britain's railways then our assessment of what needs to be done will naturally be shaped by our appreciation of what has already been achieved. Since economic historians have generally travelled the furthest in relating technical developments on the railways to wider concerns, I draw chiefly upon their analytical categories in this chapter. But I do not want to prescribe – or for that matter proscribe – any particular theoretical approach, or to suggest that economic history is the only discipline which has anything of interest to say about railways and technology. Political historians might, for example, look at how various forms of state regulation have shaped technical developments (for an initial analysis see Dobbin 1994, pp.158–212), while historians of technology have already shown how in the USA a wide range of social factors beyond those normally considered by political and economic historians affected both the rate of adoption and the physical design of certain kinds of railroad plant (for example Clark 1972). And social and cultural historians – who do not always pay as much attention as they might to technology – could profitably look more closely at the influence on people's lives of technical change on the railway (for example Robbins 1992; Jackson 1991, pp.167–203; Schivelbusch 1986; McKay 1976): the cultural symbolism of railway technologies remains a neglected topic in the British context, although one that has attracted interest in the USA (Nye 1994; Williams 1990; Danley and Marx 1990; Revill 1989). Although my own preferences will be clear, I cannot emphasize enough that a multi- and even interdisciplinary approach to the understanding of railways and technical change is the surest way of unlocking the potential of the subject for further research.

Technical Change and Productivity

One widely accepted definition of technical change describes it as the commercialization, adaptation and improvement of either production processes or products. The interest of economic historians in the phenomenon have usually focused on a series of questions concerning its genesis, diffusion and economic effects (Rosenberg 1982, pp.3–4; 1994, pp.1–23).

The effect of technical change on productivity – whether of land, labour, capital equipment or all of these – is one of the most important of these issues, and, as one of the leading technologies of the nineteenth century, railways have long been the subject of intensive research. In the 1960s Albert Fishlow's detailed econometric studies suggested that the high rate of growth in productivity of the US railroads between 1870 and 1910 was chiefly due to a reduction in costs associated with steady, incremental improvements to locomotives and freight cars, although the introduction of air brakes, automatic couplings, new signalling systems and steel rails also helped (Fishlow 1966). Reviewing the work of Fishlow and other (then) 'new economic historians', Patrick O'Brien confirmed that between about 1860 and 1890 'the technological potential for reductions in real costs was greater for railroads than for other forms of transport' (O'Brien 1977, p.36).

We have little of this sophistication on Britain's railways, although the broad chronology of developments before the First World War is clear enough. Author after author discusses changes in the materials and design of the permanent way, the development of larger, faster and more powerful locomotives, improvements to signalling and other safety devices, such as the continuous brake, and, at the end of this period, the first, cautious moves towards electrification (for example Simmons 1978, pp.142–238; Bagwell 1974, pp.76–80; Sherington 1969, pp.211–21, 259–60, 263–71). This reluctance to essay a thorough analysis of the overall cost savings to the railways or the enhanced revenue that accrued from the introduction of better passenger and freight services is understandable, for the findings of the American econometricians were severely criticized by many who pointed to significant methodological difficulties in trying to assess how much technical change contributed to improved productivity (for example Rosenberg 1982, pp.23–8; Rubin 1967). Other criticisms focused on inadequate data: also a problem in the British context since the costing and accountancy systems of railway companies prior to the First World War were notoriously slack by modern standards (Lightner 1983; Cain 1980; Aldcroft 1972; Vamplew 1972a, 1971; Irving 1971; Hawke 1970, pp.290–1, 387). For these and other reasons econometric analyses of Britain's railways have shed little light on the precise contribution of technical change to productivity growth over the long term (Vamplew 1972a; Hawke 1970, pp. 281–312; Deakin and Seward 1969, pp.192–4).[1]

There is however a place for more circumscribed inquiries into the economic consequences of technical change. Some companies in the later nineteenth and early twentieth centuries were better than others at keeping statistics, although we cannot hope for any more series as comprehensive as those of the NER, already thoroughly analysed by Bob Irving (1972, 1976). The work of Cain (1980), Irving (1984, 1978), Foreman-Peck (1990) and others over the last twenty years, that has given us a much better understanding of the capitalization, output and total factor productivity of the railways prior to 1914, could perhaps be used to attempt fresh estimates of the order of magnitude significance of technical change. Statistics are more readily available for the period after the First World War, and there remains much work to be done on the 'Big Four' (but see Crompton 1995, 1989) and even – despite Terry Gourvish's excellent appraisal of the financial implications of technical developments from 1945 to 1973 – on British Railways (BR) (Gourvish 1986). We should also remember that Britain's railways encompass more than 'the railway formerly known as BR' and its predecessors. It would be interesting to know, for example, about the differences between the engineering of BR and independent passenger railways such as London Transport; industrial railways

---

[1]   Gary Hawke and Jim Higgins later claimed that the 'impressive' productivity record of Britain's railways between 1830 and 1914 came 'mainly from improvements in the performance of assets peculiar to the railway industry'; but unfortunately they did not develop the point (Hawke and Higgins 1983, p.194).

are another neglected subject with interesting possibilities for comparative work (Lewis in this volume).

The Management and Diffusion of Technical Change

The severe difficulties facing anyone who wishes to estimate the contribution of technical change to the productivity of railways suggests that it might be wise to turn our attention to a closely related subject: the capacities of Britain's railway managers to deal with innovation. Such research should not be restricted to the nineteenth century, for firms operating in markets that were no longer unchallenged – such as the railways after the First World War – can offer interesting historical lessons in the redemptive powers of technical change (Edgerton 1996, 1987).

Business historians have of course long recognized US railroads as the nineteenth-century precursors of the large, integrated corporation, a point taken up – with suitable alterations for the differences between the two countries – by some scholars of Britain's railways (Channon 1981). But there is room for debate about the appropriate criteria against which to judge the decisions railway managers and engineers made about the technical possibilities that were open to them, and hence our more general conclusions about the nature and quality of the corporate structures of the railways and their capacity for decision making. An important aspect of work on managerial performance relating to technical change in businesses other than the railways has been the ability to compare the competitive performance of firms. But the unique nature of the railways' markets and regulatory regimes (Kirby in this volume) combine with the statistical shortcomings and methodological difficulties already noted to make this sort of comparison either otiose (when the level of competition was slight) or practically impossible for much of the railways' history.

All of this suggests that we might do better to take managerial decision making as a phenomenon amenable to historical explanation but not retrospective judgements regarding its financial efficacy. We could then move towards a less normative understanding of technical innovation than that usually assumed by business historians of railways. It is probably fair to say that a majority is still most interested in the managerial politics of companies, or their 'corporate culture', primarily from the point of view of showing how this impacted upon financial performance (for example Churella 1995; Bezilla 1980; Marx 1976). By contrast many historians of technology seek to explore how this politics shaped the very standards by which historical actors judged the success or otherwise of technical change: the absence or 'problematic' nature of statistical data thus becomes an interesting matter that requires explanation rather than a block to historical judgement. Moving towards a fuller recognition of the contested meanings of such data also implies a shift towards a richer theoretical understanding of railways, as organisations whose wider goals and purposes were open to competing definitions. One consequence is that the work of historians interested in questions of labour or gender are more readily absorbed into work on technical change (for example Drummond 1997, 1995; Brown 1995; Crompton 1989). Adopting such social constructivist approaches to the evolution of railway technologies should prove a highly fruitful line of inquiry (for example Dunlavy 1994; Usselman 1985). And because this kind of history acknowledges that individuals and personalities helped to make the past, good writing on the subject will avoid the overly abstract and dry nature of much of the existing economic history of railways.

Even if these more radical lines of inquiry are not pursued there is a need for a renewed examination and extension of some of the work undertaken by an earlier generation of economic and business historians. Their studies suggested that technical decisions were made without any clear idea of the financial, or other, benefits that might have accrued. Irving (1971) for example argued that around the turn of the century the LNWR and NER companies failed to invest in electrification partly because they did not appreciate the widespread advantages of doing so. Similarly Dyos and Aldcroft (1969, p.186) claimed that a lack of costing techniques in the workshops of the railway companies inhibited innovation in locomotive design during the nineteenth century, although the complaint is more commonly that there was too much variation and too little standardization (for example Westwood 1977). On the whole we have insufficient evidence to be sure that these conclusions apply more generally.

Take for example the area of locomotive manufacturing (Larkin and Larkin 1988). Before the First World War cost accounting was more widespread among engineering firms of all kinds in Britain than is often realized (Divall 1994), and recent studies of the private locomotive builders Beyer-Peacock shows that in the nineteenth century this company, at least, made considerable efforts to cost its products (Heap 1992; Hills and Patrick 1982). Moreover Kirby (1988) suggests that the proliferation of locomotive designs emanating from the railway companies and the privately owned workshops before the First World War resulted from a recognition of the economic advantages of continual incremental improvement. Diane Drummond has recently developed this theme, arguing that economic historians have too readily accepted the applicability to Britain's railways of criteria of technical advance evolved primarily for the analysis of the US economy. At least until 1900, she argues, British railway company workshops were as technically advanced as any in the world and their highly differentiated products and associated manufacturing techniques were well suited to the particular markets for technical labour within which the railways had to operate (Drummond 1997, pp.22–34). Indeed, John H. Brown's exemplary study (1995) of the American

Baldwin locomotive works demonstrates that this firm prospered in the nineteenth century by developing a range of products which in its diversity arguably bears comparison with that in Britain. Although there is a good deal of research currently under way on the business history of Britain's locomotive industries, much remains to be done, particularly with regard to the twentieth century. Once we move outside the charmed circle of motive power, the management of almost every area of technical change remains to be explored (but see Jenkinson 1996; Milligan 1975).

The period after the First World War has on the whole been inadequately treated. The weight of opinion, informed principally by Derek Aldcroft's pioneering studies, is still that the Big Four did not fully grasp the benefits offered by technical change, particularly when it came to the reduction of manpower and new forms of motive power (Aldcroft 1968, pp.77–83; 1974, pp.243–62; Dyos and Aldcroft 1969, pp.308–12). Interest has largely focused on traction policy; other innovations of note include standardization, particularly of rolling stock, the use of new techniques of mass production and repair, the introduction of larger capacity wagons, the cumulative effect of minor design improvements on them and on the track, and the development of new signalling and train control systems (Jenkinson 1996; Bonavia 1981, pp.83–8; Pollins 1975, pp.187–9; Aldcroft 1968, pp.77–83). A good deal of the criticism has been levelled at the management of the railways. Aldcroft, for example, while conceding that a shortage of capital meant that the Big Four were largely unable to undertake large scale electrification of the main lines in the 1920s and 1930s – a conclusion recently disputed by Crompton (1995) – felt that managers simply missed the opportunities provided by diesel traction (Aldcroft 1974, pp.247–52, 255–7).

There is scope for a critical analysis of Aldcroft's figures (see for example on the USA, McCall 1985), but a more rewarding line of inquiry might be to explore the many and varied reasons why the Big Four stayed with steam and other so-called outmoded technologies, such as low capacity wagons. Aldcroft suggested, and Michael Duffy (1982) has made a similar argument with regard to the BR standard steam locomotives in the 1950s, that engineers were simply attached to traditional ways of working; but this is merely to state the problem, not solve it. A better understanding of the corporate structures of the Big Four focusing particularly on the relationships between engineers and other senior managers would be a good starting point (for an initial analysis of the Ondon Midland & Scotish (LMS), see Divall 1998). We also need to be sensitive to the possibility that engineers and managers might have had good reasons to think that technical innovations were not as promising as they appear to us with the benefit of hindsight. These issues are rarely as straightforward as they are sometimes made out to be by those historians who lack a substantial measure of technical expertise. Michael Bonavia made a start at looking at these wider issues some years ago, pointing out that the opinions of contemporaries regarding matters such as the practicality of diesel traction and larger goods wagons were not as sanguine as Aldcroft's *post hoc* judgements: some of the disagreement concerning diesels, for example, stemmed from the issue of whether it was possible to extrapolate from the experience of North American railroads (Bonavia 1981, pp.120–38). Most histories of British motive power are too narrowly focused on technical matters to help us greatly in this task and by contrast Mark Reutter's study of the Pennsylvania Railroad's doomed attempt to stay with steam in the 1930s and 1940s shows what can be achieved by dedicated historians working outside the universities (Reutter 1994).

The thrust of the most recent work on Britain reaches similar conclusions to studies of the period before the First World War: that if there were failures to seize the full potential of new technology, the blame was in some considerable measure due to factors over which railway managers had little control (Crompton 1995). The relationship between the state and Britain's railways is as important to bear in mind in relation to technical change as it is to any other aspect of the railways' history (Kirby in this volume), a point amply demonstrated by Terry Gourvish's highly detailed history of BR (1986). While thanks to this book and the more descriptive work of John Johnson and Robert Long (1981) our understanding of the management of technical change on the nationalized railway system is considerably better than that in relation to the Big Four, case studies such as those of Stephen Potter (1987, 1993) on Britain's high speed train since the 1960s and Roxanne Powell's doctoral study (1996, 1997) of the Advanced Passenger Train and the SNCF's TGV demonstrate the value of paying close attention to both the managerial and governmental regimes under which engineers work. More work like this on the recent past might attract funding from policymakers, and although high speed trains and their associated infrastructural requirements are obvious subjects for further research, we should not ignore more mundane topics such as the development of new technologies for freight and regional and local passenger services (Whitelegg *et al.* 1993).

The Genesis of Technical Change

We readily regard recent technical change on the railways as the product of systematic research and development. But this approach to the genesis of innovation can be traced back to the late nineteenth century and by 1890 several of the larger US railroads had built laboratories for technical research (Usselman 1985, pp. 228–85). Apart however from Johnson and Long's sketch of developments since the nineteenth century (1981, pp.437–64) we have had little until recently on the history of engineering research on Britain's railways.

A comprehensive analysis of technical research undertaken by and for Britain's railways is long overdue.

I have started this task with an initial study of the LMS, chiefly because the company drew explicity upon American models of corporate organisation and technical research and so offers the potential for interesting trans-Atlantic comparisions (Divall 1998). But we must not fall into the trap of using such a narrow definition of 'research' that we are blinded to the innovative and developmental work that was done by engineers working in the traditional technical departments. As well as a more thorough examination of the LMS's engineering functions, we need comparisons with the equivalent departments on the Southern, London & North Eastern and Great Western Railways, none of which was as keen as the LMS on the American model for the organisation of research. There is of course already a large body of literature relating to these matters, but it needs to be set in the context of the facilities offered by governmental research bodies, the industrial research associations and the universities. Perhaps too someone will turn their attention to an overview of the technical research undertaken by the private manufacturers of railway locomotives, rolling stock and other equipment.

Nor should we ignore technical change on the earliest railway systems. While Lewis's magisterial study (1970) of early wooden wagonways is unlikely to be seriously revised in the light of new research, the growing interest in the technology (among other facets) of the pre-1830 railway is already causing us to think again about the respective contributions of pioneers such as George Stephenson, John Buddle and William Chapman (Rutherford 1997). Future work on particular lines and regional networks will help us to understand better the continuities and discontinuities between the essentially medieval technology of the wagonway and the sophisticated systems of the Victorian railway. A fuller grasp of the personal, business and proto-professional networks that bound together the engineers and promoters of railways in the late eighteenth and early nineteenth centuries should enhance our knowledge of the diffusion of new technologies in a period that, for all the long standing interest in the industrialization of Britain, is not as well understood as it might be; such work could also contribute to wider debates about the regional nature of industrialization.

Railways as a Cause of Technical Change in Other Industries

The influence of the railways on the development of other industries is another subject once of great interest to economic historians that would bear further examination. These 'linkages' fall into two categories: first those with industries that supplied the goods and materials used in railway construction, operation and maintenance ('backward linkages'); and secondly those with other business sectors that benefited from the expansion and integration of markets facilitated by the development of the railway system ('forward linkages'). Technical change had a part to play in both kinds of linkage, although in neither case has the issue traditionally been of the first priority.

We can deal quite briefly with forward linkages. Clearly technical change sometimes allowed for reductions in charges made for existing railway services, or for the provision of new kinds of facility entirely (faster, through goods trains for instance). In these ways the railways furthered the prosperity of other industries, and this gives us another reason for studying the technical innovations detailed earlier – if, that is, we accept this aspect of the econometric approach.[2] But there is little more to be said about forward linkages and technical change that places railways at the centre of debate. Some of the success enjoyed by non-railway businesses depended on the technologies they introduced partly in response to changing market opportunities. But the part of the railways in promoting technical change of this sort, or perhaps even in preventing it – when, for instance, a vigorous industry was debilitated by changing markets – was normally limited to their shaping of these markets. Only very occasionally do we find instances where the railways played a more direct part in promoting a new technology, for instance by offering facilities. Thus Hawke for example referred to the introduction, development and diffusion of the electric telegraph, which from the mid-nineteenth century was assisted by the granting of wayleaves by the railway companies (Hawke 1970, pp.382–4).[3]

There is one other way in which technology enters the discussion of forward linkages. In the 1960s and 1970s some econometricians were interested in the degree to which the unique technologies of railways enabled them to offer transport services that thanks to geography could not readily or economically be provided by other modes, for instance canals.[4] As O'Brien noted, judging such matters requires detailed engineering knowledge and, as several critics have pointed out, this is precisely what was lacking in much of the econometric analyses (O'Brien 1977, pp.74–5; Robbins 1991, pp.84–5). Moreover the very notion of technical change emphasizes the point that railways were developing systems, and on the whole this point was also ignored by the econometricians. There might therefore be some point to looking again at their global

---

[2] Hawke (1970, pp.381–2) makes clear which of these benefits are counted within the concept of the railways' 'social saving' and which are properly externalities to be counted among the forward linkages; but this need not concern us here.

[3] Hawke (1970, pp.382–4) played down the significance of these wayleaves, claiming that they could have been established at minimal extra cost to the telegraph companies without the assistance of the railways; but a more rounded account would also acknowledge the (unquantifiable) part played by the early use of the electric telegraph by railways in establishing its technical reliability. This aided its diffusion throughout Britain (Kieve 1973).

[4] Fogel's 'embodied benefits'.

assumptions regarding the comparative technical advantages of railways over other forms of transport, perhaps extending the period of study into the twentieth century (for an initial analysis see Evans 1981). But such an analysis would resonate more readily with the concerns of the present generation of historians if it were to try to understand the 'success' or 'failure' of different modes of transport in the context of the socio-technical factors prevailing at particular times and in particular locales. As Jack Simmons pointed out forty years ago in a study of the survival of horse traction on Britain's railways, what is regarded an outmoded kind of technology in one context might well be a sensible choice in a different set of circumstances (Simmons 1994, pp.11–22).

Backward linkages

Technical change featured a little more prominently in the analysis of backward linkages, where debates focused primarily on the iron, steel, and mechanical engineering industries. As we have come to expect, the literature on North America is much more extensive than that on Britain. Generally speaking commentators on Europe have had little cause to disagree with David Landes' view that it is 'doubtful' whether the impact of the railways on technical change in these industries was as 'consistently favourable' as that on output (Landes 1969, p.153).

　　Until very recently the case of the ferrous metal industries seemed to bear this account out. Hawke unequivocally concluded that before 1870 the demand of the English and Welsh railways for rails played no significant part in the change from iron to steel manufacture, nor in advances in finishing techniques such as the rolling of rails (1970, pp.232, 234, 243, 245; see also Hawke and Higgins 1983, pp.193–4; Gourvish 1980, pp.22–3). Reviewing the evidence from America and a number of European countries in addition to Britain, O'Brien was even more sweeping. He suggested that the railways had 'little to do' with advances in metallurgical technologies throughout the nineteenth century, although he did note Fishlow's contention that technical change in the US steel industry might have been systematically linked with railroads (O'Brien 1977, pp.65–6). For O'Brien the point was 'not likely' to be resolved because economic historians did not agree on what counted as a cause of technical innovation; in so far as it was expressed demand, the 'sales to the railroads constituted part of the environment that stimulated research into new technology for basic metallurgy.' Similarly the demand of the railways for rails might have assisted in the diffusion of known techniques throughout the iron and steel industries of Europe and North America (O'Brien 1977, pp.66–7). Alternatively, it might have allowed the continued use of technologies, such as the Bessemer process of steel manufacture in Britain from the 1880s, which would otherwise have been uneconomic (Musson 1978, p.175). Apparently there was little more to be said.

Since we need not restrict ourselves to the theoretical assumptions of these economic historians we do not have to be so pessimistic about the value of further research. Recent work on the steel industry demonstrates that there is enormous scope for exploring the ways in, and the mechanisms through which the requirements of the railways affected other industries. Thomas Misa has recently argued that in the USA the industry-wide standards adopted in the 1870s for the chemical constitution of steel produced by the Bessemer process 'owed much to the railroads': they 'selected and defined' the properties of steel to ensure that 'the metal that best filled their specific technological needs would be uniformly available' (Misa 1995, pp.1–43).

Yet for the earlier generation of historians specificities such as these counted against the railways. Fogel, for instance, said that in the USA the Bessemer process was used for little else other than the manufacture of rails, and hence that the contribution of the railways to technical innovation in the steel industry counted for little when it came to manufacturing processes of a wider economic significance. But this argument is set up in such a way that the railroads can never win. If we find that they only encouraged technical change that was specific to their own requirements, then the railroads stand condemned of producing nothing of general value for the economy. If however it turns out that technical advances adduced by the railroads were of wider relevance then it is open for economic historians to argue that the role of the railways was contingent, not necessary: the demand from firms in some other industry could have caused the technical changes which as a matter of historical fact the railroads brought about. Thus, for example, although in the USA the iron structural I-beam evolved from railway rails (Jewett 1967, 1969), it might be argued counterfactually that in the absence of railroads similar beams would have been developed by other means.

As far as research on Britain is concerned the degree of our ignorance concerning the technical influence of the railways on other industries is for the most part so great that we need not worry too much about the niceties of this sort of counterfactual argument. Detailed studies such as Misa's carried out in the British context would be very welcome, with due caution for the differences as well as the similarities between the two countries already indicated by the initial work being done on railways and the steel industry (Brooke 1986; see also Drummond 1995, pp.47–8, 101–4; Tweedale 1987; Reed 1982, pp.63, 67–73; Wengenroth 1994). Similarly Gourvish's comment (1980, pp.23, 25) that we need more studies of the impact of the railways on the technical development of the iron industry may be extended to most of those other industries – non-ferrous metals, bricks, timber and other building materials, and coal – of which he noted generally we have little knowledge.[5] There is also scope for more work on nineteenth-century developments in prime movers (but see Hills 1989) and the telegraph (Kieve 1973), while the wider impact of many of the heterogeneous techniques employed by civil engineers (earthworks, tunnels, bridges, other structures and so on) remain to be explored (Sutherland 1997). Once we move into the twentieth century, the whole field of heavy (Byatt 1979, pp.46–66) and light electrical engineering opens up including, for example, the contribution of the railways to control systems and data processing – a consequence of improvements in the regulation of motive power and rolling stock – and safety-critical systems such as signalling.

Only in the realm of mechanical engineering has a satisfactory start been made. Historians have been interested for many years in the part of the railways in promoting novel techniques in the working and handling of metal, particularly by machines, and we have a general idea about how the division of markets between company workshops and private manufacturers affected the growth of standardization in locomotives and rolling stock (Kirby 1991, 1988; Rolt 1986, pp.117–18; Saul 1970, pp.145–50; Dyos and Aldcroft 1969, pp.185–7). But only recently have more detailed studies by historians interested in the labour process enabled us to assess some of the claims made by an older generation of historians: most notably Drummond's work on the railways' workshops at Crewe and elsewhere (Drummond 1997, 1995, 1989, 1987). Much needed doctoral studies of the independent locomotive builders should shortly produce further answers. However a more general assessment of the contribution of the railways to the diffusion of new technologies and techniques awaits further studies at the level of the firm: at the moment we can do little more than echo O'Brien's point that it would be 'surprising to find that some of the solutions to technical problems posed by the railways for metallurgy, thermodynamics and the manufacture of machine tools had no spin-offs to other parts of the engineering industry' (O'Brien 1977, p.70).

Technology Transfer – Britain's Railways Abroad

Although I have drawn heavily upon North American studies to suggest subjects and approaches for future research on Britain's railways, I have not discussed at any length the potential of comparative studies. These are

---

[5] Hawke said that there is 'no reason' to suppose that railways contributed directly to the techniques of preserving wood, nor that there were any 'dependent technical advances in a "stone industry" ', although he cites little evidence for these claims. This observation with regard to wood seems particularly unwise given the interest of the railways in, for example, preserving sleepers. He admitted that the case of bricks 'is a little more uncertain' (1970 pp.211–12).

particularly relevant to the issue of the transfer of railway technologies from one country to another. For much of the nineteenth and well into the twentieth century Britain was of course a major supplier of railway technologies, technical expertise and personnel across the globe (Inkster 1991, pp.150, 177–9, 224–5; Ville 1990, pp.144–53; Buchanan 1989, pp.148–60, 1986, pp.501–24; Henderson 1972, pp.64, 69–70, 135–6, 158–9), although the influence of British ideas on European engineers was perhaps not as long lived as is commonly supposed. In the recent past the flow has tended to be in the other direction with, for instance, US diesel locomotives appearing in Britain in the 1980s and wagon technology from the same country in the late 1990s, although we can of course find much earlier instances of the importation of foreign technologies and electric tramways and railways are good examples (Yuzawa 1985; McKay 1976, pp.35–83). Current developments in the field of high-speed trains promise interesting further problems for students of technology transfer (Powell 1996, 1997; Puffert 1993).

There has been surprisingly little detailed historical work done on the fate of British railway technology exported overseas, or indeed on that of foreign equipment imported into Britain. The general questions asked in relation to other kinds of technology transfer are often relevant to railways (Fox 1996; Jeremy 1992, 1991). What for instance are the conditions which maximize the chances of such transfers being successful? What effects do the imported technologies have on the recipient country – and indeed on the exporter? In what ways does the need to function in a new environment – socially and economically as well as physically – mean that the technology alters its physical form?

This last is one of the more interesting questions currently engaging historians of technology that is relevant to the future study of railways. We are all familiar with the fact that the first British locomotives exported to the USA rapidly proved unsuitable for the lightly laid and tortuous permanent way and had to be radically modified to give a satisfactory performance. Economic historians have long argued that the design of British locomotives was specific to the economic conditions of their country of origin, where the saving of land in the construction of railways was more important than that of either capital or labour. This resulted in superbly engineered but expensive lines, and locomotives of a similar kind to run on them. By contrast in North America land was cheap, or free, but labour and capital were not. Railways were thus cheaply constructed and poorly aligned, needing a very different design of locomotive. The engines were also cheaper to build than British ones: shortages of capital forced indigenous manufacturers to standardize and adopt a form of mass production (Brown 1995; White 1994, 1979; Habakkuk 1962, pp.32–3, 87–90). Although some research is currently being undertaken on British locomotives in

Sweden there is plenty of scope for comparative work of this kind on other countries (Karlsson 1994).

As with other areas of the study of technical change, recent comparative work tends to draw upon a wider range of explanatory factors than the specifically economic. For example Eda Kranakis has shown how before 1900 the different attitudes of French and American engineers towards mathematical forms of analysis and systematic practical experimentation contributed to the markedly more successful evolution and diffusion of the steam injector, a French invention, in the USA (Kranakis 1989). Colleen Dunlavy's nuanced and sophisticated analysis of how the social, political and economic differences between Prussia and the USA were reflected in the development of their railways in the 1830s and 1840s includes much on technical change that should inspire similar comparisons for Britain (Dunlavy 1994).

Concluding Remarks

Clearly there is no shortage of theoretical perspectives or empirical studies of other countries' railways upon which we can draw inspiration for our new research agenda. In concluding I should like briefly to make just two points.

First we are fortunate in Britain to have such a large number of people outside the universities with an interest in the history of railways. There is enormous potential for academic and lay historians together to develop a rigorous and sophisticated account of technical change and Britain's railways. The evolution of 'local history' in recent years suggests that, at its best, such a partnership can produce nuanced studies that move beyond a microscopic or parochial intellectual outlook to become genuinely microcosmic in scope. Tightly focused studies that are nevertheless informed by an awareness of wider debates can provide the evidence needed to support or refute more generalized accounts, and can contribute to further theoretical work. By contrast mere detail can all too often prove to be beside the point, and unfortunately this is a problem with a considerable proportion of the writing produced by lay historians. Yet while there are undoubtedly many lessons which lay historians, and their publishers, can learn from academics, the point works the other way round as well. Academics have no monopoly over historical insights or knowledge, as I know from my own work. While undertaking research on the approach of the LMS to technical research, by chance I discussed with a retired railway worker the costing of locomotive repairs. He pointed out to me that the booked figures often bore little resemblance to the costs incurred: something which had never struck me and yet which has an obvious bearing on our ability to estimate the productivity of technical change. A small point in itself perhaps, but an important one that could be multiplied many times over.

Secondly, I should like to enter a plea for all historians to think more about the potential of forms of evidence other than traditional written sources. Oral accounts are hardly novel in the wider realm of historical scholarship but there is scope for their more widespread and better informed use in connection with railways. Physical remains, or the 'material culture', of railways, be they in museums, on heritage railways or elsewhere, might also serve more as sources of evidence. There are one or two examples of studies of extant locomotives in the USA which help us to understand, for instance, the development of the skills and techniques of railway manufacturing (White 1981). Historical archaeology can sometimes surprise us: our knowledge of the sources of supply of components to the early locomotive industry has recently been modestly extended through the examination of boiler tubes recovered from a shipwreck off Scotland, and the remarkable discovery of extensive remains of wooden wagonways at Lambton D pit in Co. Durham will surely deepen our understanding of the technology of railways in the 18th century. While discoveries of this quality are likely to be extremely rare, the extensive collections of the National Railway Museum remain under-exploited. A large and well-documented series of permanent way castings from Crewe works could, for example, tell us more about the nature of iron and steel manufacturing throughout the latter half of the 19th century. Clearly, the skills of the archaeo-metallurgist would be essential here, but as I remarked earlier such interdisciplinarity should surely be welcomed.[6] The heterogeneity of railways as sociotechnical systems requires such an eclectic approach, and is precisely what makes research on technical change such a potentially rewarding subject.

---

[6] If material objects are to be of any use to historians as evidence then curators and other custodians must give much more attention than hitherto to conserving and recording any changes to the objects in their care (Hopkin 1994, pp.215–21).

Bibliography

Aldcroft, Derek H. (1968), *British Railways in Transition: The Economic Problems of British Railways since 1914*, London: Macmillan.

Aldcroft, Derek H. (1972), 'Railways and economic growth: a review article', *Journal of Transport History*, (2nd ser.) 1 (2), September, pp.238–49.

Aldcroft, Derek H. (1974), *Studies in British Transport History 1870–1970*, Newton Abbot: David and Charles.

Anderson, B. L. and Wynn, R. F. (1975), 'The equity market and U.K. railway investment, 1831–1850', *Recherches Economiques de Louvain*, xli, pp.219–33.

Anderson, James (1801), 'On cast-iron railways', *Recreations in Agriculture, Natural-History, Arts and Miscellaneous Literature*, 4 (3), pp.198–217.

Andrews, G. H. (1853), *Rudimentary Treatise on Agricultural Engineering*, London: John Weale.

Appleton, J. H. (1962), *Geography and Communications in Great Britain*, Oxford University Press.

Bagwell, P. S. (1974), *The Transport Revolution from 1770*, London: Routledge.

Bagwell, P. S. (1988), *The Transport Revolution 1770–1985*, London: Routledge.

Barker, T. C. (1986), 'Some thoughts on the railways' competition in general and road transport competition in particular', *Journal of the Railway & Canal Historical Society*, 28, pp.328–35.

Barker, T. C. and Savage, C. I. (1975), *An Economic History of Transport in Britain*, London: Huntingdon.

Barman, C (1950), *An Introduction to Railway Architecture*, London: Art and Technics.

Baxter, B. (1966), *Stone Blocks and Iron Rails*, Newton Abbot: David and Charles.

Baxter, R.D. (1866), 'Railway extension and its results', *Journal of the Royal Statistical Society*, 29, pp.549–95.

Bennett, Alfred Rosling (1927), *The Chronicles of Boulton's Siding*, London: Locomotive Publishing Co.

Bennett, G., Clavering, E., and Rounding, A. (1990), *A Fighting Trade: Rail Transport in Tyne Coal 1600–1800*, 2 vols, Gateshead: Portcullis Press.

Bezilla, Michael (1980), *Electric Traction on the Pennsylvania Railroad 1895–1968*, University Park Pennsylvania and London: Pennsylvania State University Press.

Biddle, G. (1993), 'The railway stations of John Livock and T.M. Penson', *Journal of the Railway and Canal Historical Society*, 31 (2), p.154; and (1996) 32 (2), p.164.

Bonavia, Michael R. (1981), *Railway Policy Between the Wars*, Manchester University Press.

Booth, Adrian (1995), *Small Mines of South Wales*, Oakham: Industrial Railway Society.

Boucher, C. T. (1968), *James Brindley Engineer 1716–1772*, Norwich: Goose.

Bowskill, D. (1986), *North East Waterways*, St Ives: Imray Laurie Norie and Wilson.

Briggs, M. S. (1950), 'Sir William Tite, MP', *The Builder*, 13 and 20 January.

Bristol University Library, Brunel's Private Letter Book.

Broadbridge, S. A. (1955), 'The early capital market: the Lancashire & Yorkshire Railway', *Economic History Review*, (2nd ser.) 8, December, pp.200–12.

Broadbridge, S. A. (1957), 'The Finances of the Lancashire & Yorkshire Railway', unpublished London Ph.D thesis.

Broadbridge, S. R. (1974), *The Birmingham Canal Navigations 1768–1846*. Newton Abbot: David and Charles.

Brooke, David (1986), 'The advent of the steel rail, 1857–1914', *Journal of Transport History*, (3rd ser.) 7 (1), March, pp.18–31.

Brown, John H. (1995), *The Baldwin Locomotive Works*, Baltimore and London: Johns Hopkins University Press.

Buchanan, R. Angus (1986), 'The diaspora of British engineering', *Technology and Culture*, 27 (3), July, pp.501–24.

Buchanan, R. Angus (1989), *The Engineers: A History of the Engineering Profession in Britain 1750–1914*, London: Jessica Kingsley.

Builder, The (1935), Obituary, CXLIX (483), 13 September.

Byatt, I. C. R. (1979), *The British Electrical Industry: The Economic Returns to a New Technology*, Oxford: Clarendon Press.

Cain, P. J. (1972), 'Railway combination and government 1900–1914', *Economic History Review*, (2nd ser.) 25 (4), November, pp.623–41.

Cain, P. J. (1980), 'Private enterprise or public utility? Output, pricing, and investment in English and Welsh railways, 1879–1914', *Journal of Transport History*, (3rd ser.) 1 (1), March, pp.9–28.

Cain, P. J. (1988), 'Railways 1870–1914: the maturity of the private system', in M. J. Freeman and D. H. Aldcroft (eds.), *Transport in Victorian Britain*, Manchester University Press, pp.92–133.

Cairncross, A. K. (1953), *Home and Foreign Investment, 1870–1913*, Cambridge University Press.

Carter, E. F. (1959), *The Historical Geography of Railways in the British Isles*, London: Cassell.

Carter, O. (1995), 'Francis Thompson, 1808–1895 – an architectural mystery solved', *Backtrack*, 9, April, p.4.

Chadwick, G. F. (1985), 'Henry Hunt and the Architecture of the Eastern Counties Railways', unpublished essay.

Chandler, Alfred D. (1990), *Scale and Scope: The Dynamics of Industrial Capitalism*, Cambridge, Mass: Belknap Press.

Chandler, T. J. (1957), 'Communications and a coalfield: a study of the Leicestershire and South Derbyshire Coalfield', *Transactions Institute of British Geographers*, 23, pp.163–73.

Chandler, T. J. (1958), 'The canals of Leicestershire: their development and trade', *East Midland Geographer*, 2 (10), pp.27–40.

Channon, G. (1972), 'A nineteenth century investment decision: the Midland Railway's London extension', *Economic History Review*, (2nd ser.) 25 (3), August, pp.448–70.

Channon, Geoffrey (1981), 'A. D. Chandler's "visible hand" in transport history', *Journal of Transport History*, (3rd ser.) 2 (1), March, pp.53–64.

Churella, Albert J. (1995), 'Corporate culture and marketing in the American railway locomotive industry: American locomotive and electro-motive respond to dieselization', *Business History Review*, 69 (2), Summer, pp.191–229.

Clapham, J. H. (1964), *An Economic History of Modern Britain*, vol. i (new impr.), Cambridge University Press.

Clark, Charles H. (1972), 'The development of the semiautomatic freight-car coupler, 1863–1893', *Technology and Culture*, 13 (2), April, pp.170–208.

Clinker, C. R. and Hadfield, C. (1958), 'The Ashby de la Zouch Canal and its railways', *Transactions of the Leicestershire Archaeological & Historical Society*, 34, pp.53–76.

Compton. H. J. (1976), *Oxford Canal*, Newton Abbot: David and Charles.

Conder, F. R. (1983), *The Men who Built Railways* (orig. *Personal Recollections of English Engineers*, 1868), ed. J. Simmons, London: Thomas Telford.

Cook, R. A. and Clinker, C. R. (1984), *Early Railways between Abergavenny and Hereford*, Oakham: Railway & Canal Historical Society.

Cook, R. M. (1979), 'Archaic Greek trade: three conjectures', *Journal of Hellenic Studies*, 99, pp.152–3.

Cossons, N. (1994), 'Railway preservation: whither or wither?', *Steam Railway*, January, p.26.

Cottrell P. L. (1976), 'Railway finance and the Crisis of 1866', *Journal of Transport History*, (new ser.) 3, pp.201–41.

Course, E. (1987), Letters to RIBA library, Sancton Wood file, July and November.

Crompton, Gerald (1989), 'Squeezing the pulpless orange: labour and capital on the railways in the Inter-War Years', *Business History,* 31 (2), April, pp.66–83.

Crompton, Gerald (1995), 'The railway companies and the nationalisation issue, 1920–1950' in R. Millward and J. Singleton (eds), *The Political Economy of Nationalisation in Britain 1920–1950,* Cambridge University Press, pp.116–43.

Crouzet, F. (ed.) (1972), *Capital Formation in the Industrial Revolution,* London: Methuen.

Crowquill, A. (1849), *How He Reigned and How He Mizzled: A Railway Raillery,* London: Methuen.

Danley, S. and Marx, L. (eds) (1990), *The Railroad in American Art: Representations of Technology and Change,* Cambridge, Mass.: MIT Press.

Deakin, B. M. and Seward, T. (1969), *Productivity in Transport: A Study of Employment Capital, Output Productivity and Technical Change,* Cambridge University Press.

Deane, P. and Cole, W. A. (1964), *British Economic Growth, 1688–1959,* Cambridge University Press.

Delany, D. R. (1973), *The Grand Canal of Ireland,* Newton Abbot: David and Charles.

Delany, V. T. H. and Delany, D. R. (1966), *The Canals of the South of Ireland,* Newton Abbot: David and Charles.

Dendy Marshall, C. F. (1938), *A History of British Railways down to 1830,* Oxford University Press.

Dendy Marshall, C. F. (1953), *A History of Railway Locomotives down to the End of the Year 1831,* London: Locomotive Publishing Co.

Divall, Colin (1994), 'Professional organisation, employers and the education of engineers for management: a comparison of mechanical, electrical and chemical engineers in Britain, 1897–1977', *Minerva,* 32 (3), Autumn, pp.241–66.

Divall, Colin (1996), 'What kind of railway (engineering) history should we be writing?' in A. Jarvis (ed), *Approaches to Engineering History,* Liverpool: Merseyside Maritime Museum and the Newcomen Society, pp.19–27.

Divall, Colin (1998), 'Down the American road? Industrial research on the London, Midland and Scottish Railway, 1923–1947' in J. Armstrong, C. Bouneau, and J. Vidal Olivares (eds), *Railway Management,* Aldershot: Scolar Press, forthcoming.

Dixey, S. J. (1994), 'Charles Trubshaw, a Victorian railway architect' in

Bedside Backtrack, Penryn: Atlantic Publishing, and subsequent correspondence with author.

Dobbin, Frank (1994), *Forging Industrial Policy: The United States, Britain and France in the Railway Age*, Cambridge University Press.

Dow, G. (1962), *Great Central*, vol. 2, London: London Locomotive Publishing Co. Ltd.

Drummond, D. (1989),' "Specifically designed"? employers' labour strategies and worker responses in British railway workshops, 1838–1914', *Business History*, 31 (2), April, pp.8–31.

Drummond, Diane K. (1987), 'Building a locomotive: skill and the workforce in Crewe locomotive works, 1843–1914', *Journal of Transport History*, (3rd ser.) 8 (1), March, pp.1–29.

Drummond, Diane K. (1995), *Crewe: Railway Town, Company and People, 1840–1914*, Aldershot: Scolar Press.

Drummond, Diane K. (1997), 'Technology and the labour process: a preliminary comparison of British railway companies' approaches to locomotive construction before 1914' in Colin Divall (ed), *Perspectives on Railway History: Papers Delivered at the SHOT Meeting, London, August 1996*, York: Institute of Railway Studies, pp.22–34.

Duckham, B. F. (1983), 'Canals and river navigations' in D. H. Aldcroft and M. F. Freeman (eds), *Transport in the Industrial Revolution*, Manchester University Press, pp.100–41.

Duffy, Michael C. (1982), 'Technomorphology and the Stephenson traction system', *Transactions of the Newcomen Society*, 54, pp.55–78.

Duncan, I. G. T. (1981), *Navigable Waterways of Nottinghamshire: A Survey in Industrial Archaeology*, Nottingham: Nottingham University Department of Adult Education/WEA East Midlands Branch.

Dunlavy, Colleen (1994), *Politics and Industrialization: Early Railroads in the United States and Prussia*, Princeton, NJ: Princeton University Press.

Dyos, H. J. and Aldcroft, D. H. (1969), *British Transport: An Economic Survey from the Seventeenth Century to the Twentieth*, Leicester University Press.

Dyos, H. J. and Aldcroft, D. H. (1974), *British Transport: An Economic Survey from the Seventeenth Century to the Twentieth*, Harmondsworth: Penguin.

Edgerton, D. E. H. (1987), 'Science and technology in British business history', *Business History*, 29 (4), October, pp.84–103.

Edgerton, D. E. H. (1996), *Science, Technology and British 'Decline'*, Cambridge University Press.

Edgeworth, Richard Lovell (1813), *An Essay on the Construction of Roads and Carriages*, London: J. Johnson.

Elbaum, Bernard and Lazonick, William (eds) (1987), *The Decline of the*

British Economy, Oxford: Clarendon Press.

Elton, Arthur (1963), 'The Pre-history of railways', *Proceedings of Somersetshire Archaeological and Natural History Society*, 107, pp.31–59.

Engineer, The, 11 July 1879, pp.31, 34

Etherington, A. Roy, Excell, Peter S. and Tonks, Eric S. (1969), *British Industrial Locomotives*, (1st ed) Great Sutton: Industrial Railway Society.

Evans, Francis T. (1981), 'Roads, railways and canals: technical choices in 19th-century Britain', *Technology and Culture* 22 (1), January, pp.1–34.

Evans, G. H. (1936), *British Corporation Finance, 1775–1850*, Baltimore: Johns Hopkins University Press.

Everitt, A. (1973), 'Town and country in Victorian Leicestershire: the role of the village carrier', in A. Everitt (ed), *Perspectives in English Urban History*, London: Macmillan, pp.213–40.

Everitt, A. (1976), 'Country carriers in the nineteenth century', *Journal of Transport History*, 3, pp.179–202.

Faulkner, A. H. (1972), *Grand Junction Canal*, Newton Abbot: David and Charles.

Feinstein, C. H. (1961), 'Income and investment in the United Kingdom, 1856–1914', *Economic Journal*, 71, pp.367–85.

Fishlow, Albert (1965), *American Railroads and the Transformation of the Ante-Bellum Economy*, Cambridge, Mass.: Harvard University Press.

Fishlow, Albert (1966), 'Productivity and technological change in the railroad sector, 1840–1910' in National Bureau of Economic Research, *Output, Employment, and Productivity in the United States after 1800*, London: NBEC/Columbia University Press, pp.583–646.

Fogel, Robert W. (1964), *Railroads and American Economic Growth: Essays in Econometric History*, Baltimore: Johns Hopkins University Press.

Foreman-Peck, J. and Millward, R. (1994), *Public and Private Ownership of British Industry 1820–1990*, Oxford: Clarendon Press.

Foreman-Peck, James (1990), 'Railways and Late Victorian growth' in James Foreman-Peck (ed), *New Perspectives on the Late Victorian Economy: Essays in Quantitative Economic History 1860–1914*, Cambridge University Press, pp.73–95.

Fox, F. (1904), *River, Road and Rail*, London: John Murray.

Fox, Robert (ed.) (1996), *Technological Change: Methods and Themes in the History of Technology*, Amsterdam: Harwood Academic.

Franks, D. L. (1975), *Ashby & Nuneaton Railway*, Sheffield: Turntable Publications.

Freeman, M. J. (1983), 'Introduction' in D. H. Aldcroft and M. J. Freeman (eds), *Transport in the Industrial Revolution*, Manchester University Press, pp. 1–30.

Freeman, M. J. (1988), 'Introduction' in M. J. Freeman and D. H. Aldcroft (eds), *Transport in Victorian Britain*, Manchester University Press, pp. 1–56.

Freeman, M. J. and Aldcroft, D. H. (1985), *The Atlas of British Railway History*, London: Croom Helm.

Freeman, M. J. and Aldcroft, D. H. (eds) (1988), *Transport in Victorian Britain*, Manchester University Press.

Fullerton, B. (1975), *The Development of British Transport Networks*, Oxford University Press.

Gale, W. K. V. (1975), *A History of the Pensnett Railway*, Cambridge: Goose and Son.

Gayer, A. J., Rostow, W. W. and Schwartz, A. J. (1953), *The Growth and Fluctuation of the British Economy, 1790–1850*, Oxford: Clarendon Press.

Gee, Chris (1993), 'Trafford Park Estate railway into the 1990s', *Industrial Railway Record*, 134, pp. 165–76.

Goodchild, John (1977), *The Lake Lock Rail Road*, Wakefield: Metropolitan District Libraries.

Goodwin, D. (1987), '1894 plans: Bertram William Cook', *Union: Journal of the Old Union Canals Society & Foxton Incline Plane Trust*, 80, pp. 10–11.

Goodwin, D. (1988), *Foxton Locks and the Grand Union Canal Company*, Desborough: Foxton Inclined Plane Trust.

Gourvish, T. R. (1972), *Mark Huish and the London and North Western Railway: A Study of Management*, Leicester University Press.

Gourvish, Terence R. (1980), *Railways and the British Economy 1830–1914*, London: Macmillan.

Gourvish, Terence R. (1986), *British Railways: A Business History*, Cambridge University Press.

Gourvish, Terence R. (1993), 'What kind of railway history did we get? Forty years of research', *Journal of Transport History*, (3rd ser.) 14 (2), September, pp. 115–25.

Gray, Thomas (1820), *Observations on a General Iron Rail-way*, London: Baldwin, Cradock and Joy (and subsequent editions; anonymous until 1825 edn).

Grenter, Stephen (1993), 'A wooden waggonway complex at Bersham Ironworks, Wrexham', *Industrial Archaeology Review*, 15, pp. 195–207.

Habakkuk, H. J. (1962), *American and British Technology in the Nineteenth Century*, Cambridge University Press.

Hadfield, C. (1966), *The Canals of the East Midlands*, Newton Abbot: David and Charles.

Hadfield, C. (1984), *British Canals: an Illustrated History*, Newton Abbot: David and Charles.

Hadfield, C. and Biddle, G. (1979), *Canals of North West England*, Newton Abbot: David and Charles.

Hadfield, Charles (1960), *The Canals of South Wales and the Border*, Cardiff: University of Wales Press.

Hadfield, Charles and Skempton, A. W. (1979), *William Jessop, Engineer*, Newton Abbot: David and Charles.

Hall, Edmund Hyde (1952), *A Description of Caernarvonshire (1809–1811)*, ed. Emyr Gwynne Jones, Caernarvon: Caernarvonshire Historical Society.

Harris, N. (1994), 'Editorial', *Steam Railway*, January, p.6.

Hatley, V. A. (1970), *Rails over Blisworth Hill: The Story of Northamptonshire's first railway*, Northampton Historical Series, 2.

Havilland, John de (1994), *Industrial Locomotives of Dyfed and Powys*, London: Industrial Railway Society.

Hawke, G. R. and Reed, M. C. (1969), 'Railway capital in the United Kingdom in the nineteenth century', *Economic History Review*, (2nd ser) 22, pp.269–86.

Hawke, G. R. (1970), *Railways and Economic Growth in England and Wales 1840–1870*, Oxford: Clarendon Press.

Hawke, Gary and Higgins, Jim (1983), 'Britain' in P. O'Brien (ed), *Railways and the Economic Development of Western Europe 1830–1914*, London: Macmillan, pp.170–202.

Haworth, B (1994), 'Inspiration and investigation: four great railway engineers', in D. Smith (ed), *Perceptions of Great Engineers: Fact and Fantasy*, London: Science Museum, pp.65–72.

Heap, Christine (1992), 'Nineteenth-century production and pricing at Beyer, Peacock & Company, locomotive manufacturers, Manchester' in N. Cossons, A. Patmore and R. Shorland-Ball, (eds), *Perspectives on Railway History and Interpretation*, York: National Railway Museum, pp.23–37.

Henderson, W. O. (1972), *Britain and Industrial Europe 1750–1870*, (3rd ed.), Leicester University Press.

Highland Railway (1913), *List of the Shareholders of the Highland Railway Company at 1st December 1913*, Inverness.

Hillier, K. (1984), *The Book of Ashby de la Zouch*, Buckingham: Barracuda Books.

Hills, Richard (1989), *Power from Steam: A History of the Stationary Steam Engine*, Cambridge University Press.

Hills, Richard and Patrick, D. (1982), *Beyer, Peacock: Locomotive Builders to the World*, Glossop: Transport Publishing.

Hindley, Philip G. (1980), 'The Penmaenmawr quarry inclines', *Industrial Railway Record*, 86, pp.173–94.

Hodgkiss, D. J. (1978), 'Cromford & High Peak Railway', *Journal of the Railway & Canal Historical Society*, 24, pp.25–31.

Holt, G. (1992), *The Ticknall Tramway*, Ticknall: Ticknall Preservation & Historical Society.

Hopkin, Dieter (1994), 'A commentary on restoration, conservation and the National Railway Museum Collection' in R. Shorland-Ball (ed), *Common Roots – Separate Branches: Railway History and Preservation*, London: Science Museum/National Railway Museum, pp.215–21.

Hudson, Graham S. (1971), *The Aberford Railway and the History of the Garforth Collieries*, Newton Abbot: David and Charles.

Hughes, J. R. T. (1960), *Fluctuations in Trade, Industry and Finance: A Study of British Economic Development, 1850–1860*, Oxford: Clarendon Press.

Hughes, Stephen (1990), *The Brecon Forest Tramroads: the Archaeology of an Early Railway System*, Aberystwyth: Royal Commission on Ancient and Historical Monuments in Wales.

Industrial Locomotive Society (1967), *Steam Locomotives in Industry*, Newton Abbot: David and Charles.

Inkster, Ian (1991), *Science and Technology in History: An Approach to Industrial Development*, London: Macmillan.

Irving, R. J. (1971), 'British railway investment and innovation 1900–1914', *Business History*, 13 (1), January, pp.39–63.

Irving, R. J. (1976), *The North Eastern Railway: An Economic History*, Leicester University Press.

Irving, R. J. (1978), 'The profitability and performance of British Railways, 1870–1914', *Economic History Review*, (2nd ser.) 31 (1), February, pp.46–66.

Irving, R. J. (1984), 'The capitalisation of Britain's Railways, 1830–1914', *Journal of Transport History*, (3rd ser.) 5 (1), March, pp.1–24.

Jackson, Alan A. (1991), *Semi-Detached London: Suburban Development, and Transport, 1900–39*, (2nd edn), Didcot: Wild Swan.

Jenkinson, David (1996), *British Railway Carriages of the 20th Century*, (2nd ed.) Penryn: Atlantic Transport Publishers.

Jeremy, David J. (ed) (1991), *International Technology Transfer: Europe, Japan and the USA 1700–1914*, Aldershot: Edward Elgar.

Jeremy, David J. (ed.) (1992), *The Transfer of International Technology: Europe Japan and the USA in the Twentieth Century*, Aldershot: Edward Elgar.

Jewett, Robert A. (1967), 'Structural antecedents of the I-beam, 1800–1850', *Technology and Culture*, 8 (3), July, pp.346–62.

Jewett, Robert A. (1969), 'Solving the puzzle of the first American structural I-beam', *Technology and Culture*, 10 (3), July, pp.371–91.

Johnson, John and Long, Robert A. (1981), *British Railways Engineering 1948–80*, London: Mechanical Engineering Publishing.

Johnston, C, and Hume, J. R (1979), *Glasgow Stations*, Newton Abbot: David and Charles.

Karlsson, Lars O. (1994), 'Purchase or adaptive redevelopment: the British locomotive in Sweden' in R. Shorland-Ball (ed), *Common Roots – Separate Branches: Railway History and Preservation*, London: Science Museum/National Railway Museum, pp.95–100.

Kellett, J. R. (1969), *The Impact of Railways on Victorian Cities*, London: Routledge and Kegan Paul.

Kenwood, A. G. (1965), 'Railway investment in Britain, 1825–1875', *Economica*, (new ser.) 32, pp.313–22.

Keynes, J. M. (1973), *The General Theory of Employment, Interest and Money*, London: Royal Economic Society edn.

Kidner, R. W. (1994), 'Passenger carriages on tramroads', *Journal of the Railway & Canal Historical Society*, 31 (6), pp.313–16.

Kieve, J. L. (1973), *The Electric Telegraph: A Social and Economic History*, Newton Abbot: David and Charles.

Kirby, M. W. (1993), *The Origins of Railway Enterprise: the Stockton and Darlington Railway, 1821–1863*, Cambridge University Press.

Kirby, Maurice W. (1988), 'Product proliferation in the British locomotive building industry, 1850–1914: an engineer's paradise?', *Business History*, 30 (3), July, pp.287–305.

Kirby, Maurice W. (1991), 'Technological innovation and structural division in the UK locomotive building industry 1850–1914' in Colin Holmes and Alan Booth (eds), *Economy and Society: European Industrialisation and Its Social Consequences*, Leicester University Press, pp.24–42.

Kirkaldy, A. W. and Evans, A. D. (1924), *The History and Economics of Transport*, (3rd edn), London: Pitman.

Kranakis, Eda (1989), 'Social determinants of engineering practice: a comparative view of France and America in the 19th century', *Social Studies of Science*, 19 (1), February, pp.5–70.

Landes, David S. (1969), *The Unbound Prometheus: Technological Change and Industrial Development in Western Europe from 1750 to the Present*, Cambridge University Press.

Larkin, Edgar J. (1979), *Memoirs of a Railway Engineer*, London: Mechanical Engineering Publishing.

Larkin, Edgar J. and Larkin, John G. (1988), *The Railway Workshops of Britain*, London: Macmillan.

Le Guillou, M. (1975), 'Freight rates and their influence on the Black Country iron trade in a period of growing domestic and foreign competition, 1850–1914', *Journal of Transport History*, (new ser.) 3 (2), pp.108–18.

Lee, Charles E. (1943), *The Evolution of Railways*, (2nd edn), London: Railway Gazette.

Lewin, J. (ed) (1981), *British Rivers*, London: Allen and Unwin.

Lewis, M. J. T. (1970), *Early Wooden Railways*, London: Routledge.

Lewis, M. J. T. (1975), 'Steam on the Penydarren', *Industrial Railway Record*, 59, pp.1–36.

Lewis, M. J. T. (1996), 'Archery and Spoonerisms: the creators of the Ffestiniog Railway', *Journal of the Merioneth Historical and Record Society*, 12 (3), pp.263–76.

Lewis, M. J. T. and Denton, J. H. (1974), *Rhosydd Slate Quarry*, Shrewsbury: Cottage Press.

Lightner, D. L. (1983), 'Railroads and the American economy: the Fogel thesis in retrospect', *Journal of Transport History*, (3rd ser.) 4 (2), September, pp.20–34.

Lindsay, J. (1968), *The Canals of Scotland*, Newton Abbot: David and Charles.

Lindsay, J. (1979), *Trent & Mersey Canal,* Newton Abbot: David and Charles.

Lodge, Trevor (1994), 'A Midland branch in south Yorkshire', *Industrial Railway Record*, 136, pp.245–59.

McCall, John B. (1985), 'Dieselisation of American railroads: a case study', *Journal of Transport History,* (3rd ser.) 6 (2), September, pp.1–17.

MacDermot, E. T. (1964), *History of the Great Western Railway*, vol. 1, (rev. C. R. Clinker), London: Ian Allan.

MacDonald, Brian R. (1986), 'The Diolkos', *Journal of Hellenic Studies*, 106, pp.191–5.

McKay, John P. (1976), *Tramways and Trolleys: The Rise of Urban Mass Transport in Europe*, Princeton, NJ: Princeton University Press.

Mahon, G. R. (1961), 'Railways and bogs in Ireland', *Journal of Transport History*, 5 (2), pp.116–26.

Marshall, A. (1919), *Industry and Trade*, London: Macmillan.

Marshall, J. (1982), *Cromford & High Peak Railway*, Newton Abbot: David and Charles.

Marx, Thomas G. (1976), 'Technological change and the theory of the firm: the American locomotive manufacturing industry, 1920–1955', *Business History Review*, 50 (1), Spring, pp.1–24.

Matthews, R. C. O. (1954), *A Study in Trade-Cycle History: Economic*

Fluctuations in Great Britain, 1833–1842, Cambridge University Press.

Mellor, R. E. H. (1969), *Geography of the USSR: Transport,* Wellington: Hicks Smith and Sons.

Mellor, R. E. H. (1979), *German Railways: A Study in the Historical Geography of Transport*, Aberdeen: Department of Geography, University of Aberdeen, O'Dell Memorial Monograph 8.

Mellor, R.E.H. (1995), *Railways in Britain: An Historical-Geographical Perspective,* Aberdeen: Department of Geography University of Aberdeen O'Dell Memorial Monograph 26.

Mercer, H. (1995) *Constructing a Competitive Order: The Hidden History of British Antitrust Policies*, Cambridge University Press.

Messenger, Michael J. (1978), *Caradon and Looe: the Canal, Railways and Mines*, Truro: Twelveheads Press.

Miller, M. G. and Fletcher, S. (1984), *The Melton Mowbray Navigation,* Oakham: Railway and Canal Historical Society.

Milligan, John (1975), *The Resilient Pioneers: A History of the Elastic Rail Spike Company and Its Associates*, Aberdeen, Edinburgh and London: Paul Harris Publishing.

Misa, Thomas (1995), *A Nation of Steel: The Making of Modern America 1865–1925*, Baltimore and London: Johns Hopkins University Press.

Mitchell, B. R. (1964), 'The coming of the railway and United Kingdom economic growth', *Journal of Economic History*, 24, pp.315–36.

Morgan, D. (1993), *Steam Railway*, December, p.21.

Morriss, R. K. (1983), *Railways of Shropshire,* Shrewsbury: Shropshire Libraries.

Mountford, Colin E. and Charlton, L. G. (1977), *Industrial Locomotives of Durham*, Market Harborough: Industrial Railway Society.

Mulholland, Peter (1978), 'The first locomotive in Whitehaven,' *Industrial Railway Record*, 75, pp.177–9.

Murphy, M. (1994), 'New insights into the Mackenzie Collection', in D. Smith (ed), *Perceptions of Great Engineers: Fact and Fantasy*, London: Science Museum, pp.85–91.

Musson, A. E. (1978), *The Growth of British Industry*, London: Batsford.

Newby, N. (1994), *Steam Railway*, February, p.22.

Nolan, John and Durkin, Andrew (1996*), The Wooden Wagonway at the Former Lambton Cokeworks and D Pit Site*, Newcastle: City of Newcastle Archaeology Unit.

Nye, David (1994), *The American Technological Sublime,* Cambridge, Mass. and London: MIT Press.

O'Brien, Patrick (1977), *The New Economic History of the Railways*, London: Croom Helm.

O'Dell, A. C. (1956), *Railways and Geography,* London: Hutchinson.

O'Dell, A. C. and Richards, P. S. (1971), *Railways and Geography.* London: Hutchinson.

Oeynhausen, C. von, and Dechen, H. von (1971), *Railways in England, 1826 and 1827*, trans. E. A. Forward, ed. Charles E. Lee and K. R. Gilbert, Cambridge: Newcomen Society.

P[arliamentary] P[apers] 1850 XXXI, Report of the Commissioners of Railways.

P[arliamentary] P[apers] 1882 XIII, Select Committee on Standing Orders [167].

P[arliamentary] P[apers] 1902 XC, Return...of shareholders [HC 400].

Parker, J. H. (1980), 'Ten years of change', *Industrial Railway Record*, 84, pp.116–19.

Parris, H. (1965), *Government and the Railways in Nineteenth Century Britain*, London: Routledge and Kegan Paul.

Patmore, J. A. (1964), 'The railway network of the Manchester conurbation', *Transactions of the Institute of British Geographers*, 34, pp.159–73.

Paxton, R. (1990), *100 years of the Forth Bridge*, London: Thomas Telford.

Payne, E. M. S. (1961), *The Two Jameses and the Two Stephensons, or the Earliest History of Passenger Transit on Railways*, repr. 1861, Dawlish: David and Charles.

Peacock, Thomas B. (1952), *P. L. A. Railways*, London: Locomotive Publishing Co.

Pellow, T. (1985), *The Shroppie: a Portrait of the Shropshire Union Main Line and its Middlewich Branch*, Crewe: Landscape Press.

Phillips, Sir Richard (1814), 'A morning's walk from London to Kew,' *Monthly Magazine*, 38, September, p.119.

Pollins, H. (1952), 'The finances of the Liverpool and Manchester Railway', *Economic History Review*, (2nd ser.) 5, pp.90–7.

Pollins, H. (1954), 'The marketing of railway shares in the first half of the nineteenth century', *Economic History Review*, (2nd ser.) 7, pp.230–9.

Pollins, H. (1957–8), 'Railway contractors and the finance of railway development in Britain', *Journal of Transport History*, 3, pp.41–51, 103–10.

Pollins, H. (1971), *Britain's Railways: An Industrial History*, Newton Abbot: David and Charles.

Potter, Stephen (1993), 'Managing High Speed Train projects' in J. Whitelegg, S. Hulten and T. Flink (eds), *High Speed Trains: Fast Tracks to the Future*, Hawes: Leading Edge, pp.145–61.

Potter, Stephen (1987), *On the Right Lines? The Limits of Technological Innovation*, London: Frances Pinter.

Powell, E. Roxanne (1996), 'The Frontiers of State Practice in Britain and France: Pioneering High Speed Rail Technology and Infrastructure

(1965–1993)', Unpublished Ph.D thesis, London School of Economics and Political Science.

Powell, E. Roxanne (1997), 'APT and TGV: two conceptions of modern railway engineering 1965–1985', in Colin Divall (ed.), *Perspectives on Railway History: Papers Delivered at the SHOT Meeting, London, August 1996*, York: Institute of Railway Studies, pp.35–59.

Pratt, E. A. (1912), *A History of Inland Transport and Communication*, repr. 1970, Newton Abbot: David and Charles.

Priestland, P. (ed.) (1989), *Radcliffe on Trent 1837–1920: A Study of a Village During an Era of Change*, Radcliffe on Trent: Ashbracken.

Puffert, Douglas J. (1993), 'Technical diversity: the integration of the European High Speed Train network' in J. Whitelegg, S. Hulten and T. Flink (eds), *High Speed Trains: Fast Tracks to the Future*, Hawes: Leading Edge, pp.162–71.

Railway News (1914), 'British railway stocks: over 20,000,000 beneficial holders', in *The Jubilee of the Railway News*, London.

Railway Returns...for the year 1906 [Cd 3705, 1907].

Railway Times (1865), pp.1166, 1226.

Ransom, P. J. G. (1996), *Narrow Gauge Steam: Its Origins and World-wide Development*, Sparkford: Oxford Publishing Co.

Rattenbury, Gordon (1980), *Tramroads of the Brecknock and Abergavenny Canal*, Oakham: Railway & Canal Historical Society.

Rattenbury, Gordon (1982), 'Cwm Dee Rail Road', *Journal of the Railway & Canal Historical Society*, 27 (5), pp.98–102.

Rattenbury, Gordon (1983), 'Penllwyn Tramroad', *Journal of the Railway & Canal Historical Society*, 27 (7), pp.189–97.

Rattenbury, Gordon (1988), 'Hall's Tramroad', *Journal of the Railway & Canal Historical Society*, 29 (4), pp.170–183.

Rattenbury, Gordon (1989), 'The Trevil Railroad Co', *Journal of the Railway & Canal Historical Society*, 29 (9), pp.454–69.

Rattenbury, Gordon, and Cook, Ray (1996), *The Hay and Kington Railways*, Mold: Railway & Canal Historical Society.

Redman, R. N. (1972), *The Railway Foundry, Leeds, 1939–1969*, Norwich: Goose & Son.

Reed, Brian (1982), *Crewe Locomotive Works and its Men*, Newton Abbot: David and Charles.

Reed, M. C. (1968), 'George Stephenson and W. T. Salvin: the early railway capital market at work', *Transport History*, i, pp.10–20.

Reed, M. C. (1975), *Investment in Railways in Britain, 1820–1844: A study in the Development of the Capital Market*, Oxford University Press.

Reutter, Mark (1994), 'The great (motive) power struggle: the Pennsylvania Railroad v. General Motors, 1935–1949', *Bulletin of Railroad History*, 170, Spring, pp.15–33.

Revill, George (1989), 'Paternalism, Community and Corporate Culture: A Study of the Derby Headquarters of the Midland Railway Company and its Workforce 1840–1900', unpublished Ph.D thesis, Loughborough University.

Reynolds, P. R. (1979), *The Brecon Forest Tramroad*, Swansea: Author.

Reynolds, P. R. (1980), 'Scott's tramroad, Llansamlet', *Journal of the Railway & Canal Historical Society*, 26 (3), pp.85–95.

Riden, P. J. (1973), 'The Butterley Company and railway construction, 1790–1830', *Transport History*, 6 (1), pp.30–52.

Rimmer, A. (1985), *The Cromford & High Peak Railway*, Headington: Oakwood Press.

Robbins, Michael (1957), 'What kind of railway history do we want?', *Journal of the Railway & Canal Historical Society*, 3 (10) p.22; revised version, in *Journal of Transport History*, 3 (1957), pp.65–75, and (retitled 'The railway historian's craft') in Michael Robbins, *Points and Signals*, London: Allen and Unwin (1967), pp.18–31.

Robbins, Michael (1991), 'The progress of transport history', *Journal of Transport History*, (3rd ser.) 12 (1), March, pp.74–87.

Robbins, Michael (1992), 'Railway electrification in London and its social effects' in N. Cossons, A. Patmore and R. Shorland-Ball (eds), *Perspectives on Railway History and Interpretation*, York: National Railway Museum, pp.48–57.

Rolt, L. T. C. (1971), *The Making of a Railway*, London: Hugh Evelyn.

Rolt, L. T. C. (1986), *Tools for the Job: A History of Machine Tools to 1850*, (2nd edn), London: Science Museum.

Rosenberg, Nathan (1982), *Inside the Black Box: Technology and Economics*, Cambridge University Press.

Rosenberg, Nathan (1994), *Exploring the Black Box: Technology, Economics and History*, Cambridge University Press.

Rostow, W. W. (1960), *The Stages of Economic Growth: A Non-Communist Manifesto*, Cambridge University Press.

Royal Commission on Canals & Inland Waterways (1907), *Volume 3: Evidence and Appendices*, London: HMSO [Cd. 3718].

Royal Commission on Canals & Inland Waterways (1909), *Volume 5 (Part 2): Minutes of Evidence*, London HMS0, [Cd. 4840].

Royal Commission on Canals & Waterways 1910, *Volume 7: Fourth and Final Report: England & Wales and Scotland*, London HMSO, [Cd. 4979].

Rubin, J. (1967), Review of Fogel (1964), *Technology and Culture*, 8 (2), April, pp.228–34

Rutherford, Michael (1997), 'In the beginning', *Backtrack* 11 (10), October, pp.539–45.

Saul, S. B. (1970), 'The market and the development of the mechanical engineering industries 1860–1914' in S. B. Saul (ed), *Technological Change: the United States and Britain in the Nineteenth Century*, London: Methuen, pp.141–70.

Schivelbusch, Wolfgang (1986), *The Railway Journey: The Industrialization of Space and Time in the 19th Century*, Leamington Spa: Berg.

Scrivenor, H. (1849), *The Railways of the United Kingdom Statistically Considered*, London: Smith, Elder and Co.

Sheeran, G. (1994), *Railway Buildings of West Yorkshire 1812–1920*, Keele: Ryburn Publishing.

Sherington. C. E. R. (1934), *A Hundred Years of Transport 1830–1933*, London: Duckworth.

Sherington, C. E. R. (1969), *A Hundred Years of Inland Transport 1830–1933*, London: Frank Cass.

Shill, Ray (1989), 'Invitations to tender', *Industrial Railway Record*, 119, pp.54–62.

Simmons, J. (1978), *The Railway in England and Wales, 1830–1914*, Leicester University Press.

Simmons, J. (1986), *The Railway in Town and Country*, Newton Abbot: David and Charles.

Simmons, J. (1991), *The Victorian Railway*, New York: Thames and Hudson.

Simmons, J. (ed.) (1986), *The Railways of Britain*, London: Macmillan.

Simmons, Jack (1978), *The Railway in England and Wales 1830–1914: The System and Its Working*, Leicester University Press.

Simmons, Jack (1994), *The Express Train and Other Railway Studies*, Nairn: Thomas & Lochar.

Siviour, G. R. (1974), 'The changing relationship between railways and the iron industry and steel industry in the East Midlands', *East Midland Geographer*, 6, pp.29–39.

Skempton, A. W. and Andrews, A. (1976–77), 'Cast iron edge-rails at Walker Colliery 1798', *Transactions of the Newcomen Society*, 48, pp.119–22

Smiles, S. (1862), *Lives of the Engineers: George and Robert Stephenson*, London: John Murray.

Smith, A. (1848), *The Bubble of the Age or, the Fallacies of Railway Investments, Railway Accounts, and Railway Dividends*, (3rd edn), London: Sherwood, Gilbert and Piper.

Smith, David L. (1967), *The Dalmellington Iron Company, its Engines and Men*, Newton Abbot: David & Charles.

South Eastern Railway (1860), *List of Stockholders, 1 March 1860*, London.

Spackman, W. F. (1843), *Statistical tables...of the United Kingdom of Great Britain and its Dependencies...*, London: Longman.

Spencer, H. (1854), 'Railway morals and railway policy', *Edinburgh Review*, C, 204, October, pp.420–61

Spencer, K. M. (1977), 'Railways and the turnpikes in Preston 1830–1850', *Transport History*, 8, pp.45–53.

Stevens, P. A. (1992), *The Leicester and Melton Mowbray Navigation*, Stroud: Alan Sutton/ Leicestershire County Council.

Stevenson, P. (1970), *The Nutbrook Canal: Derbyshire*, Newton Abbot: David & Charles.

Sutherland R. J. M. (ed.) (1997), *Structural Iron, 1750–1850*, Aldershot: Ashgate.

Tann, Peter (1996), 'The Tappenden Tramroad to the Neath Canal, 1800–14', *Journal of the Railway & Canal Historical Society*, 32 (2), pp.88–102.

Taylor, A. J. (1972), *Laissez-faire and State Intervention in Nineteenth Century Britain*, London: Macmillan.

Termin, Peter (1975), *Causal Factors in American Economic Growth in the Nineteenth Century*, London: Macmillan.

Tew, D. (1984), *The Melton to Oakham Canal*, Sycamore Press, Wymondham.

Tipper, Rev. D. A. (1975), *Stone and Steam in the Black Mountains*, Littleborough: Author.

Tomlinson, J. (1994), *Government and the Railway Enterprise since 1900*, Oxford: Clarendon Press.

Tomlinson, W. W. (1915), *The North Eastern Railway: Its Rise and Development*, repr. 1967 with an introduction by Ken Hoole, Newton Abbot: David and Charles.

Tonks, Eric S. (1959), *The Ironstone Railways and Tramways of the Midlands*, London: Locomotive Publishing Co.

Tonks, Eric S. (1988–92), *The Ironstone Quarries of the Midlands: History, Operations and Railways*, 9 vols, Cheltenham: Runpast.

Tooke, T. and Newmarch, W. (1838–57), *A History of Prices*, vols 4–5, London: P. S. King and Son.

Townley, C. H. A., Smith, F. D., and Peden, J. A. (1991–92), *The Industrial Railways of the Wigan Coalfield*, 2 vols, Cheltenham: Runpast.

Turnbull, G. L. (1969), 'The railway revolution and the carriers' response: Messrs Pickford & Co, 1830–1850', *Transport History*, 2, pp.48–71.

Turnock, D. (1990), *Railways in the British Isles: Landscapes Land Use and Society*, Newton Abbot: David & Charles.

Turnock, D. (1997), *The Canals of Leicestershire and their Impact on the Landscape*, Leicester: Leicester University Department of Geography, Occasional Paper 37.

Turnock, D. (1998), *An Historical Geography of Railways in Great Britain and Ireland*, Aldershot: Scolar Press.

Tweedale, Geoff (1987), *Sheffield Steel and America: A Century of Commercial and Technological Interdependence*, Cambridge University Press.

Usselman, Steven W. (1984), 'Air brakes for freight trains: technological innovation in the American railroad industry, 1869–1900', *Business History Review*, 58 (1), Spring

Usselman, Steven W. (1985), 'Running the machine: the management of technological innovation on American railroads, 1860–1910', unpublished Ph.D thesis, University of Delaware.

Vamplew, Wray (1971a), 'Railways and the transformation of the Scottish economy', *Economic History Review*, (2nd ser.) 24, February, pp.37–54.

Vamplew, Wray (1971b), 'Nihilistic impressions of British railway history' in D. N. McCloskey (ed), *Essays on a More Mature Economy: Britain After 1840*, London: Methuen, pp.345-58.

Vamplew, Wray (1972a), 'Railways and the Scottish transport system in the nineteenth century', *Journal of Transport History*, (new ser.) 1, February, pp.133–45.

Vamplew, Wray (1972b), 'Scottish railways and the development of the Scottish locomotive building industry in the nineteenth century', *Business History Review*, 46 (3), Autumn, pp.320–38.

Ville, Simon P. (1990), *Transport and the Development of the European Economy, 1750–1918*, London: Macmillan.

Wahl, Jürgen (1993), 'Três Minas: Vorbericht über die archäologischen Ausgrabungen im Bereich des römischen Goldbergwerks 1986/7', in Heiko Steuer and Ulrich Zimmermann (eds), *Montanarchäologie in Europa*, Sigmaringen: Jan Vorbeke Verlag.

Weaver, Rodney (1983), 'Ancient Britons', *Industrial Railway Record*, 96, pp.89–96.

Wengenroth, Ulrich (1994), *Enterprise and Technology: The German and British Steel Industries 1865–1895*, Cambridge University Press.

Westwood, J. N. (1977), *Locomotive Designers in the Age of Steam*, London: Sidgwick and Jackson.

White, John H. (1979), *A History of the American Locomotive: Its Development: 1830–1880*, (2nd edn) New York: Dover and Constable.

White, John H. (1981), *The John Bull: 150 Years a Locomotive*, Washington: Smithsonian Institution.

White, John H. (1985), *The American Passenger Car*, 2 vols., (2nd ed.), Baltimore and London: Johns Hopkins University Press.

White, John H. (1993), *The American Freight Car*, Baltimore and London: Johns Hopkins University Press.

White, John H. (1994), 'Old debts and new visions: the interchange of ideas in railway engineering' in R. Shorland-Ball, (ed.), *Common Roots – Separate Branches: Railway History and Preservation*, London: Science Museum/National Railway Museum, pp.65–87.

Whitelegg, J., Hulten, S. and Flink, T. (eds) (1993), *High Speed Trains: Fast Tracks to the Future*, Hawes: Leading Edge.

Wilkes, L. (1980), *John Dobson, Architect and Landscape Gardener*, Appendix, Stocksfield: Oriel Press.

Willan, T. S. (1936), *River Navigation in England 1600–1750*, Oxford University Press.

Williams, Rosalind (1990), *Notes on the Underground*, Cambridge, Mass. and London: MIT Press.

Wilson, E. A. (1975), *The Ellesmere & Llangollen Canal: An Historical Background*, Chichester: Phillimore.

Wood, W. W. & Stamp, J. (1928), *Railways*, London: Butterworth.

Yuzawa, Takeshi (1985), 'The introduction of electrical railways in Britain and Japan', *Journal of Transport History*, (3rd ser.) 6 (1), March, pp.1–22.

INDEX

Aberdeen, 46
    University of, xvi
Abergavenny, Mon, *see* canals: individual
    canals and navigations
Aberford, Yorkshire, *see* tramroads: *by*
    place.
accounting, cost, 101; *see also* railways
Acts of Parliament *see* Parliament, Acts
Adams, William Bridge, *see* railways:
    locomotives, engines: builders
agriculture, agricultural sector, 13, 21, 83,
    85
    produce, 87
airfields, construction of, 85
Alma Park Camp, Grantham, Lincs, 47
America, North, 33, 35, 106, 108, 109;
    see also railways
Anderson, James, 85
Anderton, Ches, 40
apprenticeship, 14
archaeo-metallurgists, 111
archaeology, 66, 93, 94, 111
architects, engineers and engineering, 65,
    66, 72, 73, 74, 75
    chief, 72
    civil, 108
    resident, 72
    structural, 72; *see also* railways:
      architects, engineers
archives, records, sources, 6, 7, 77, 78,
    82, 111
    commercial, 18
    company, 7
    engineers, 82
    family, 18
    industrial, 82
    local, 18
    national, 93
    parliamentary, 7
Arklingworth, Northants, *see* canals:
    individual canals and navigations
Arley, Worcs, 63
art, fine, 66

Ashby, *see* canals: individual canals and
    navigations; railways: compa-
    nies,   *etc.*
Ashford, Kent, 73
Ashton, Northants, *see* canals: individual
    canals and navigations
Ashwell, Leics, 40
Asia, Central, 80
    Minor, 78
Association of Railway Preservation
    Societies, *see* railways: societies
Atherstone, Warwicks, 48
Athlone, 45
Athol, Duke of, 62
Audley End, Essex, 64
America, North, 33, 35, 106, 108, 109

Backtrack, *see* railways: publications
Bagnall, *see* railways: locomotives,
    engines: builders
Baldwin *see* railways: locomotives,
    engines: builders
Balkans, 78
Bangor, Caernarvon, 83
banks, banking, 16
    joint stock, 23
Barnsley, West Yorks, 90
Barry, Sir Charles, *see* railways: archi-
    tects, engineers
Bath, Som, 63, *see also* railways: sta-
    tions.
Beaufort, Mon, *see* tramroads: *by place*
Beazley, Samuel, *see* railways: architects,
    engineers
Bedford, 74
    Duke of, 74
Beechwood, *see* railways: tunnels
Bell, William, *see* railways: architects,
    engineers
Belvoir Castle, Leics, *see* tramroads: *by*
    place
Bersham, *see* railways: companies,

Dobson, John, *see* railways: architects,
    engineers
Dockray, Robert, *see* railways: architects,
    engineers
docks, 46, 72, 85
Dorchester, *see* railways: companies, *etc.*
Dover, 85
Dowlais, Glam *see* industries: iron:
    ironworks; tramroads: *by place*
droughts, 40
Dublin, 46
    Portobello, 46, *see also* railways:
      companies, *etc.*; stations
Dumbartonshire, *see* railways: compa-
    nies, *etc.*
Durham, 38, 79
    county, 80, 86, 87, 111
Dyfed, 86

East Anglia, 59
East Midlands *see* Midlands
Economic and Social Research Council
    (ESRC), xv, 1, 3
economic booms, cycles, depressions, re-
    coveries, growth, 9–11, 19
    1835–6, 17
    1840s, 14
    1844–5, 17
    1847, 11, 12
    1853, 11
    1873–96, 3
    1897–1900, 56
economic indicators, 8
economics
    laissez-faire, 21
    macro, 8, 10
    monopoly, 22, 30, *see also* Britain:
      economy
Edgeworth, Richard Lovell, 85
Edinburgh, 85, *see also* canals: individual
    canals and navigations; rail-
    ways: companies, *etc.*
education, training
    adult, 6, 95
    distance, 6
    lifelong, 6

electric tramways, 30
electricity, 21
Ellesmere Port, Ches, 45
Ellistown, Leics, 48, 49
enclosure commissioners, 84
*Encylopaedia of Cottage, Farm and
    Villa Architecture*, 74
Enfield, Kildare, 45
engineering workshops, firms, 85, 101
    Hawks Crawshay & Co., 87
engineers, *see* railways: architects,
    engineers
engines, internal combustion , 56, *see
    also* motor vehicles; railways:
    locomotives, engines
England, 10, 15, 39
    eastern, 24
    north-east, 30
    south-west, 30
    southern, 24
England, George, *see* railways: locomo-
    tives, engines
Erewash, Erewash Valley, *see* canals:
    individual companies,
    navigations; railways: compa-
    nies, *etc.*
Errington, J.E., *see* railways: contractors
Essex, Earl of, 63
estuaries *see* rivers
Eton College, 63
Europe, 3, 19, 78, 106, 109
Euston, *see* railways: stations

Falmouth, Cornwall, 85
Fens, 59
Ffestiniog, Merioneth, *see* railways:
    companies, *etc.*
Finedon, Northants, 53
fly-boats, *see* canals: boats
Forest of Dean ,*see* coal: coalfields
forestry, 85
fork lift trucks, 92
Fox, Charles,
    Fox, Francis
      Fox Henderson & Co., *see* railways:
      architects, engineers

Wrexham, Denbigh, 80
Wyatt, Matthew Digby,
    see railways: architects, engi-
    neers
Wyre, Lancs, *see* railways: companies,
    etc.

Yare, *see* rivers
Yarmouth, Norf, 85
York, 24
    University of, 3
Yorkshire, 81
    West Riding, 30, 62